ENCYCLOPAEDIA OF EMINENT THINKERS

VOLUME-II: NEHRU

Encyclopaedia of Eminent Thinkers Series

Vol. I. The Political Thought of **Mahatma Gandhi**
Vol. II. The Political Thought of **Nehru**
Vol. III. The Political Thought of **Rabindra Nath Tagore**
Vol. IV. The Political Thought of **Radhakrishnan**
Vol. V. The Political Thought of **Vinoba**
Vol. VI. The Political Thought of **Aurobindo**
Vol. VII. The Political Thought of **Jayaprakash Narayan**
Vol. VIII. The Political Thought of **Vivekananda**
Vol. IX. The Political Thought of **Ambedkar**
Vol. X. The Political Thought of **M.N. Roy**
Vol. XI. The Political Thought of **Dadabhai Naoroji**
Vol. XII. The Political Thought of **Veer Savarkar**
Vol. XIII. The Political Thought of **M.A. Jinnah**
Vol. XIV. The Political Thought of **Tej Bahadur Sapru**
Vol. XV. The Political Thought of **C. Rajagopalachari**
Vol. XVI. The Political Thought of **Subhas Chandra Bose**
Vol. XVII. The Political Thought of **Mohammad Iqbal**
Vol. XVIII. The Political Thought of **K.B. Hedgewar**
Vol. XIX. The Political Thought of **Bhagat Singh**
Vol. XX. The Political Thought of **M.S. Golwalkar**
Vol. XXI. The Political Thought of **Sir Syed Ahmed Khan**
Vol. XXII. The Political Thought of **Mahadev Govind Ranade**
Vol. XXIII. The Political Thought of **Pandit Deendayal Upadhyaya**
Vol. XXIV. The Political Thought of **Lokmanya Bal Gangadhar Tilak**
Vol. XXV. The Political Thought of **Annie Besant**
Vol. XXVI. The Political Thought of **C.R. Das**
Vol. XXVII. The Political Thought of **Gopal Krishna Gokhale**
Vol. XXVIII. The Political Thought of **Lala Lajpat Rai**
Vol. XXIX. The Political Thought of **Maulana Abul Kalam Azad**
Vol. XXX. The Political Thought of **Sir Pherozeshah Mehta**

About the Author

K.S. Bharathi did his Master's Degree in Gandhian Thought, Peace-Science, Economics, and political Science. He also did Postgraduate Diplomas in Politics, Public Administraion, Population Dynamics, Gandhian Thought, Tourism, and Telgu. He has contributed some articles in learned journals. He is the author of : *Foundation of Gandhian Thought Gandhi and Humanity, Socio Religious Thoughts of Mahatma Gandhi, The philosophy of Sarvodya, The Satyagraha of Mahatma Gandhi, Gandhi and Nehru, Foundatoins of Ambedkar Thought, The Social Philosophy of Mahatma Gandhi, Gandhian Approach to Rural Development, The Relevance of Gandhi, Gandhi and Vinoba, The Philosophical Foundations of Gandhian Thought, The Political Thought of Gandhi, The Economic Thought of Gandhi, The Social Thought of Gandhi* and *The Quintessence and Chronology of Gandhi*. At present, he is the Head of the Postgraduate Department of Gandhian Thought of Nagpur University. He is the Chairman of the Board of Studies of Gandhian Thought, member of the Academic Council, member of the Faculty of Social Science, member of the Board of Examination, and member of the Doctoral Research Committee of Nagpur University.

ENCYCLOPAEDIA OF EMINENT THINKERS

VOLUME TWO

THE POLITICAL THOUGHT OF NEHRU

K.S. BHARATHI
Head, P.G. Department of Gandhian Thought
Nagpur University, Nagpur

CONCEPT PUBLISHING COMPANY PVT. LTD.
NEW DELHI-110059

ISBN: 978-81-7022-686-4 (Vol. 2)
ISBN: 978-81-7022-684-0 (Series)

First Published 1998

Published and Printed by

Concept
Since 1974

Concept Publishing Company Pvt. Ltd.
A/15-16, Commercial Block, Mohan Garden,
New Delhi-110059 (India)
T: 91-11-41101460
E: publishing@conceptpub.com, *W*: www.conceptpub.com

TO

REKHA

PREFACE

Nehru visualised and strove for a world free from strife, where the human being was free and could love with dignity. The message of peaceful co-existence was a voice of sanity in a world poised on the brink of self-destruction. The concept of non-alignment gave to international politics, a third force, which stood apart from the two power blocs and gradually gained in strength, fortified by the hopes and aspirations of millions of peace loving peoples all over the world. His firm belief in the dignity of the human being conditioned his perception of international affairs. Under the stewardship of Nehru, India was in the forefront of denouncing racialism and demanding stringent measures to isolate the racialist regime. He had visualised an India which would follow the path of democracy, socialism, secularism, and non-alignment.

The life and works of Jawaharlal Nehru has been discussed in the first chapter. His views on leadership has been covered in the second chapter. His views on Socialism and Freedom have been analysed in the third and fourth chapters. His original writings on Indian National Congress has been reproduced in the fifth chapter. His views on Religion and Politics has been discussed in the last chapter.

I would like to place on record my indebtedness to scholars and thinkers whose ideas enabled me to bring out this book. I gratefully acknowledge the scholars from whose works I have drawn citations viz. Dr. Ahluwalia, Dr. Bakshi, Dr. Bali, Dr. Bimal Prasad, Dr. Dutt, Dr. Grover, Dr. Saroj Prasad, Dr. Alexander Gorav and Pandit Jawaharlal Nehru.

So far as the writing of this book is concerned, whatever success I have achieved is due to relentless efforts and encouragement of Dr. P.S.G. Kumar, Head, Department of Library and Information Science, Nagpur University. I sincerely express my gratitude to him.

I express my warm thanks to Mr. P.N. Hardas and Mr. S.T. Patale of Nagpur University.

I am indebted to Concept Publishing Co., New Delhi for publishing this book in such a short span of time. Finally I hold myself to blame for the errors and shortcomings if any. This work would not have been completed without the grace of Lord Venkateswara of Tirumala and Alamelu Thayar of Tiruchanur.

K.S. BHARATHI

CONTENTS

1

LIFE AND WORKS OF NEHRU

The life of Jawaharlal Nehru, his thoughts and exploits, and the facts and events connected with him have become part of history and are no longer subject to change. With time, however, we become even more appreciative of the grandeur of his personality. With regard to the fulfilment of his patriotic duty, he was the national leader of India; as regards his international activities, he was an outstanding champion of peace and a political figure of a global calibre. He was an ardent Indian patriot, yet the significance of his political activities spread far beyond the boundaries of his country. His policies, humanist and moral principles had a quality that appealed to all humanity and became a phenomenon of worldwide significance. He never confined himself to politics alone. He was a man of noble character, full of inner warmth and charm, temperament and dramatism. He always retained faith in social progress, placing the basic interests of the people above momentary political gains.[1]

Being the founder of the non-aligned movement and an impassioned advocate of international solidarity among the Afro-Asian nations who had cast off the colonialist yoke, Nehru never sought national isolation or revenge. He believed in the common destiny of mankind and in East-West rapprochement. He rejected nationalism. He was an irreconcilable fighter against national strike and religious intolerance. His political legacy belongs not only to India but also to humanity as a whole. It was his conviction that the historical situation made him choose politics as a career.

Nehru dominated the Indian political scene for about half a century and was the most popular leader India has produced during modern times. His personality had a glamour, a charm which at times kept even his opponents spell-bound. Together with Gandhiji and others he fought and struggled hard for the freedom of India. He spent the best period of his youth in imprisonment. His was a life dedicated and devoted to the cause of his country. After independence, he remained the Prime Minister of India for seventeen years till his death. During this period, he raised India to an important position among nations of the world, where its voice was listened to with attention and respect. It was his sincere work for peaceful coexistence and faith in democratic socialism which made him popular with democratic nations as well as the Communist States. His efforts went a long way in lessening the tensions of world politics.[2]

Nehru was born on 14 November, 1889 in Allahabad to a family of Brahmans from Kashmir, the most aristocratic caste of Hindu society. Regarding his childhood days Nehru said, 'My childhood was thus a sheltered and uneventful one. I listened to the grown-up talk of my cousins without always understanding all of it. Often this talk related to the overbearing character and insulting manners of the English people, as well as Eurasians, towards Indians, and how it was the duty of every Indian to stand up to this and not to tolerate it. . . . I was filled with resentment against the alien rulers of my country who misbehaved, and whenever an Indian hit back I was glad .... I admired father tremendously. He seemed to me the embodiment of strength and courage and cleverness, far above all the other men I saw, and I treasured the hope that when I grew up I would be rather like him. But much as I admired him and loved him I feared him also .... I do not remember bearing any ill-will towards my father. . . . of religion I had very hazy notions. It seemed to be a woman's affair, father and my older cousins treated the question humorously and refused to take it seriously. The women of the family indulged in various ceremonies and *pujas* from time to time and I rather enjoyed them, though I tried to imitate to some extent the casual attitude of the grown-up men of the family. . . . But more than all the festivals I was interested in one annual event in which I played the central part—the celebration of the anniversary of my birth. This was a day of great excitement for me.[3]

Motilal Nehru was an exceptionally energetic person and possessed a tremendous will to live. He soon became an accomplished lawyer. Having begun his practice by collecting small fees for handling civil suits and property complaints for Indian princes, he began to receive six-figure remunerations. He bought a large castle-like house on the picturesque outskirts of Allahabad. He called his house, 'Anand Bhawan'. With his son's approval he would give the Anand Bhawan to the fighters for India's independence and the building would be renamed Swaraj Bhawan.[4] He was eager to give his son a European education. He employed a European teacher to give his son lessons at home. He wanted him to have the best education in a prestigious educational establishment in England. In 1905, he enrolled his son at Harrow.

Regarding his experiences at Cambridge, Nehru said, 'Some of the noted Indian politicians of the day visited us at Cambridge. We respected them but there was also a trace of superiority in our attitude. We felt that ours was a wider culture and we could take a broader view of things. . . . Among my contemporaries at Cambridge there were several who played a prominent part in Indian Congress politics in later years. J.M. Sen Gupta left Cambridge soon after I went up. Saifud-Din Kitchlew, Syed Mahmud and Tasadduk Ahmed Sherwani were more or less contemporaries. . . . In London also there was the student centre opened by the India office. This was universally regarded by Indians, with a great deal of justification, as a device to spy on Indian students. . . . The political situation in India had drawn my father into more active politics and I was pleased at this although I did not agree with his politics. . . . His clear thinking led him to see that hard and extreme words lead nowhere unless they are followed by action appropriate to the language. He saw no effective action in prospect. The *Swadeshi* and boycott movements did not seem to him to carry matters far. . . . I left Cambridge after taking my degree in 1910. I was only moderately successful in my science tripos examination, obtaining second class honours. . . . I came across some old Harrow friends and developed expensive habits in their company.[5]

Nehru acknowledged his debt to England openly. He said, "Personally, I owe too much to England in my mental make-up ever to feel wholly alien to her. And, do what I will, I cannot get rid of the habits of mind, and the standards and ways of judging other countries as well as life generally. All my predilections (apart from the political plane) are in favour of England and the English people, and if I have become what is called an uncompromising opponent of British rule in India, it is almost in spite of myself."[6]

Nehru had admired Buddhism all along. He said, 'The conception of the Buddha, to which innumerable loving hands have given shape in carven stone and marble and bronze, seems to symbolise the whole spirit of Indian thought, or at least one vital aspect of it. Seated on the lotus flower, calm and impassive, above passion and desire, beyond the storm and strife of this world, so far away he seems, out of reach, unattainable. Yet again we look and behind those still, unmoving features there is a passion and an emotion, strange and more powerful than the passions and emotions we have known. His eyes are closed, but some power of the spirit looks out of them and a vital energy fills the frame. The ages roll by and Buddha seems not so far away after all; his voice whispers in our ears and tells us not to run away from the struggle but, calm-eyed, to face it, and to see in life ever greater opportunities for growth and advancement.'[7]

In 1912 Nehru was called to the Bar. At the age of 23 he returned to India and enrolled himself as an advocate of the Allahabad High Court. Soon after his return to India, he attended the Bankipore Congress. In 1916 he was married to Kamala. In 1916 he met Gandhiji at the Lucknow session of the Indian National Congress. Till then he had hardly any idea about the conditions of the working people. In 1920 he met a group of farmers who had come to Allahabad and were camping on the river bank. He listened to their pathetic tale. It was thus that he became involved in the Kisan movement. After meeting these poor *kisans* he felt a sense of shame at his own easy going life. He wanted to identify himself with the masses.

In 1923 Nehru was appointed general secretary of the Congress and also he was elected the chairman of the Allahabad Municipality. He became secretary of Home Rule League, Allahabad in 1918. He was also elected to the All India Congress Committee. In 1923 he was arrested. This was the beginning of his association with the freedom struggle in the Indian states. He went to Moscow and attended the tenth anniversary of the Russian Revolution. He was impressed by the progress made by Russia in the field of education, and improvement in the lot of the peasants in Russia.

Nehru was elected the president of Congress in 1929. As Congress president, he declared that he was a socialist and a republican and not a believer in kings and princes or in the order which produced the modern kings of industry. In 1936, he openly advocated socialism. To him, socialism was something more than economic doctrine. It was a philosophy of life. It was the only way to end the poverty, the unemployment, the degradation and the subjection of the Indian people.

While always keeping to his own positions, throughout his life Nehru was tremendously influenced by Gandhiji. This was sometimes due more to Gandhiji's personality than to his philosophy. He said, "What a wonderful man was Gandhiji after all, with his amazing and almost irresistible charm and subtle power over people. His writings and his sayings conveyed little enough impression of the man behind; his personality was far bigger than they would lead one to think."[8] Though he had great regard for Gandhiji he was not a blind follower. He denounced Gandhiji's decision to attend the Second Round Table Conference of 1931. He was arrested in 1932 and was sentenced to imprisonment for two years. He was unhappy about the coming up of two political parties based on religion namely, the Muslim League for the Muslims and the Hindu Mahasabha for the Hindus. He was an ardent believer in secularism as is evident from the Karachi resolution of the Congress which was drafted primarily by him.

Nehru toured and delivered a number of speeches. He was considered as an eloquent spokesman of the liberation movement of all subjected peoples of the world. During the Second World War he wanted that India should take part in the world struggle against fascism. He was imprisoned at the fort at Ahmednagar in Maharashtra for nearly three years. In all he went to prison nine times and spent more than nine years behind bars. In July 1946, the Viceroy invited Nehru to nominate the representatives on behalf of the Congress to an Interim Government on 2 September, 1946. He became the Vice-President of the Executive Council.

In the beginning Nehru reacted strongly against any suggestion for partitioning the country. But in June, 1947, the AICC accepted partition as inevitable. On 15 August, 1947, India and Pakistan came into being as two separate independent countries. He became the first Prime Minister of free India. He served as Prime Minister for seventeen years. He devoted a great deal of time to the detailed provisions of the Constitution, and left on it the imprint of his idealism, his burning love of freedom and justice, and his devotion to peaceful change. He believed in Parliamentary democracy. He was against Rajendra Prasad's views on the Hindu Code Bill, and cooperative farming. He had differences with Sardar Patel also. After Patel's death in 1950 he controlled the government with much authority. His popularity had declined after the Chinese aggression but he still retained his supremacy over Congress affairs. He was the chief architect of India's foreign policy. He strengthened India's bonds with foreign countries.

Nehru propounded a policy of peace and non-alignment. In 1945 he enunciated the doctrine of Panchsheel. It comprised five principles, namely, mutual respect for territorial integrity and sovereignty, non-aggression, non-interference in each other's internal affairs, equality, and peaceful co-existence. He advised greater intercourse between nations and their leaders and he initiated the experiment of having personal contacts between world leaders. He supported the liberation movements in any part of the world. He was shocked and bewildered when Chinese attacked India in 1962. This weakened his position, lowered his prestige. His foreign policy came in for criticism.

Nehru was a man of scientific temper. He wanted his countrymen to participate fully in the march of science. Science, he stressed again and again, was necessary for rapid industrialisation of the country. He considered planning as the application of science to national problems. The example of planning in Russia enthused him greatly. He took active part in the proceedings of the National Planning Committee. In 1955 he had persuaded the Avadi Congress to accept the socialistic pattern of society as its goal. He believed in mixed economy. He did not speak of the wholesale expropriation of private property or of the immediate socialisation of the means of production. He wanted to follow the middle path.[9]

Nehru was not only a great leader or statesman but above all he was a great man. He was the darling of all—young or old, men or women. His love for children has become proverbial. He treated his servants as members of his family and shared their joys and sorrows. He loved not only human beings but also birds and beasts, mountains and rivers. He was also a passionate lover of books. During his imprisonment, reading was his major hobby, the only other being writing. He used to read on varied subjects—history, philosophy, politics, science etc. His works show him to be a profound thinker with boundless knowledge and diversified intellectual interests: besides political analysis, they deal with economics, literature 'art, ethics, aesthetics, mythology, religion' sociology and philosophy. His books are the result of the scrupulous work of a gifted and mature scholar, of his findings, observations and conclusions.

Nehru was a cultured man—polished and polite, totally free from prejudice and full of wit and vitality. He was sincere to his friends, devoted to his wife, affectionate to his daughter and an ideal brother. He had a keen sense of humour which was spontaneous and refreshingly original. He never allowed it to dim or diminish or rust. He looked almost angelic when in humour. He had a keen sense of duty and believed in the dignity of labour. He was a man of future. He was deeply interested in his country and was proud of his people.

Nehru can rightly be called architect of Modern India. He was of the firm opinion that without economic and social freedom, political freedom had little meaning. Constitution was relevant to him only as an instrument of social change. He was aware of the heterogeneous character of our society. He was conscious of the aspirations of the people representing different sections and interests, regions and religions. He made a major contribution in ensuring incorporation of provisions relating to various safeguards for minorities and tribal areas, their representation in the Parliament and the principle of equality in the Constitution of India. This he felt was necessary to bring all the ethnic, lingual and religious groups in the national stream and instil in them a sense of oneness and belonging. The objectives resolution which he moved in the Constituent Assembly on 13 December, 1946 guaranteed justice, social, economic and political; equality of status, opportunity and before the law; freedom and thought, expression, belief, faith, worship, vocation, association and action, to the people of India.

Nehru was very clear in his vision that the Modern India should radiate scientific temper which includes freedom from every form of fundamentalism and respect for universal values of human dignity. He deprecated hatred for other person's faith and emphasised the need to evolve a secular outlook. He emphasised that democracy and secularism are the basis on which India's unity could be achieved and maintained. His idea of national integration through secularism requires a careful look in the prevalent socio-political, inter-religious and inter-caste conflicts in India. He broadened the concept of secularism with reference to the Indian society where caste is a permanent cause of class divisions and privileges. He held that a caste ridden society is not properly secular. He did not wish to interfere with anybody's personal beliefs but emphasised that where these beliefs become petrified in caste divisions, undoubtedly they affect the social structure of the state. So, secularism implied elimination of all social inequalities.[10]

Nehru looked upon agriculture as a vital part of the Indian economy. In 1963, he said, "I am all for industry, I am all for steel plants, heavy industries and all that, but I do say agriculture is far more important than industry, because it is out of the success of agriculture that industry comes. If you fail in agriculture, you have little to stand upon. Where do you get the wherewithal to have industry? It is out of the surplus from agricultural production that you build your industries and therefore it has become of the utmost importance that agriculture should flourish and should produce the goods and surplus needed for industrial growth."[11]

Nehru believed that a strong industrial base is vital for the rapid economic growth of Indian economy. He was of the opinion that India possessed vast natural resources and substantial manpower potentials. He believed that India's economic development could be achieved only through modern industrialisation. He was not opposed to the development of agriculture or cottage and small scale industries; rather he laid great stress on the development of agriculture and small scale industries in the true Gandhian spirit. He contended that the development of other sectors of the Indian economy are directly correlated to the development of modern heavy industries and application of modern science and technology. He was aware of the consequences of his own line of thought and action in the matter of heavy industrialisation. He did not lay emphasis on the development of employment-oriented small scale sector besides the large scale industries in the private as well as public sector. He wanted to work for self-sufficiency in food, clothing, housing.

Nehru was in favour of modern means of transport and many other developments. He said, "If that is so, inevitably a measure of heavy industries exists. How far that will fit in with a purely village society? Personally I hope that heavy or light industries should all be decentralised as far as possible and this is feasible now because of development of electric power. If two types of economies exist in the country there would be either conflict between the two or one will overwhelm the other."[12] Regarding industrialisation, he said, "Industrialisation is an expensive job to begin with. It swallows up money without any return for some time. Unless plenty of money is available, either by loan or otherwise, it results in poverty and distress till such time as the industry begins to work and make money. England was extraordinarily fortunate in getting these vast sums of money from India just when she wanted them most for her developing industries and factories. In spite of these contradictions, however, the capitalist form of civilisation taught many a useful lesson. It taught organisation for the big industries and large scale industry require a great deal of organisations before they can function. It taught cooperation in large undertakings. It taught efficiency and punctuality. It is not possible to run big factories or a railway system unless these qualities are present."[13]

To have state control over key industries Nehru advocated nationalisation. To him, the most important objective was to increase production and nationalisation was only a means to achieve that end. He said, "If nationalisation adds to production, we shall have nationalisation at every step. If it is does not, let us see how to bring it about in order not to impede production."[14] He did not wish to go for nationalisation in blind way. He did not regard socialism as synonymous with nationalisation. He did not accept the idea that a kind of general scheme of nationalisation would bring about greater equalisation. He was in favour of the rapid industrialisation of India so that she could be relieved of pressure on land, combat poverty and raise her standards of living, her defence and a variety of other purposes.

Nehru went to Bhubaneshwar in January 1963 to attend the session of the All India Congress Committee. There he suffered a mild heart attack. He did not take proper rest but continued to work as before. On 27 May, 1963 he was suddenly taken ill in the morning and died peacefully at 2 p.m. To quote Dr. Zakir Hussain, "Nehru was a rock on which we built faith in ourselves. An aristocrat by birth and temperament, Shri Nehru had committed himself totally and unequivocally to democratic ideals, democratic institutions and democratic procedure. . . Shri Nehru worked for peace with such conviction and such deep sincerity that he became one of the pioneer architects of an emerging peaceful world community. He gave our foreign policy a direction which, let us hope, will contribute significantly to the full realisation of peace on our planet."[15]

Mr. Harold Wilson, leader of the British Labour Party, in a message to the President of India described Mr. Nehru as a dedicated fighter for freedom and democracy. He said, "His (Nehru) wisdom has given India the advantage of a magnificent heritage. With his help India brought a new voice, a voice of principle, into the councils of the world. To India belongs the pride of producing a leader of such stature but it is the whole world, not India alone which is diminished by his death."[16]

C. Rajagopalachari paid a glowing tribute. He said, "Eleven years younger than me, eleven times more important for the nation, and eleven hundred times more beloved of the nation Shri Nehru has suddenly departed from our midst and I remain alive to hear the sad news from Delhi-and bear the shock. Shri Nehru was ill and knew it was a serious form of illness, but we did not imagine he would be snatched away so unceremoniously and so swiftly."[17]

President Radhakrishnan declared, 'Nehru was one of the greatest figures of our generation, and an outstanding statesman whose services to the cause of human freedom are unforgettable. As a fighter for freedom he was illustrious, as a maker of modern India his services were unparalleled. His life and work have had a profound influence on our mental make-up, social structure and intellectual development. It will be difficult to reconcile ourselves to the image of India without Nehru's active and all-pervasive leadership. An epoch in our country's history has come to a close."[18] Mrs. Indira Gandhi said, "The story of Jawaharlal Nehru is that of a man who evolved, who grew in storm and stress till he became the representative of much that was noble in his time. It is the story of a generous and gracious human being who summed up in himself the resurgence of the 'third world' as well as the humanism which transcends dogmas and is adopted to the contemporary context."[19]

REFERENCES

1. Alexander Gorev, *Jawaharlal Nehru*, pp. 5-7.
2. B.K. Ahluwalia and S. Ahluwalia, *Architects of Swaraj*, p. 127.
3. Jawaharlal Nehru, *An Autobiography*, pp. 6-9.
4. Alexander Gorev, *Jawaharlal Nehru*, pp. 13-14.
5. Jawaharlal Nehru, *An Autobiography*, pp. 22-25.
6. *Ibid.*, p. 419.
7. Jawaharlal Nehru, *The Discovery of India*, pp. 142-43.
8. Jawaharlal Nehru, *An Autobiography*, p. 508.
9. K.S. Bharathi, *Gandhi and Nehru*, pp. 23-25.
10. I.P. Massey, *Nehruvian Constitutional Vision*, pp. 24-26.
11. K.S. Bharathi, *Gandhi and Nehru*, p. 63.
12. Shriman Narayan, *Towards Gandhian Plan*, pp. 67-68.
13. Jawaharlal Nehru, *Glimpses of World History*, p. 365.
14. Jawaharlal Nehru, *Independence and After*, p. 164.
15. K. S. Bharathi, *Gandhi and Nehru*, p. 26.
16. *Ibid.*, p. 26-27.
17. *Ibid.*, p. 27.
18. *Ibid.*
19. *Ibid,*

2

ON LEADERSHIP

Nehru was not only a valiant fighter for the freedom of his country, a model of selfless devotion to a cause, and an indefatigable crusader for social justice but also a champion on the world stage of peaceful co-existence, of equality of nations, of dignity of the oppressed humanity, and of a world free of exploitation. In all these fields, he will be remembered for generations to come.

The period between 1947 and 1964 can be described as the Nehru Era. By the time India emerged as an independent country and Nehru assumed office as its first Prime Minister he had already acquired a certain social and political outlook and also developed a certain style of leadership which continued to determine the nature of his role as the undisputed leader of independent India for about seventeen years. It was his active participation in the non-cooperation movement in 1920-21 under Gandhiji's leadership which for the first time brought him face to face with the Indian masses, made him conscious of their poverty and prepared the ground for his fascination for socialism. In 1926-27, in Europe, he came in contact with the main currents of radical thought and movement there, particularly through participation in the Brussels Congress of Oppressed Nationalities and visit to the Soviet Union. He said, "Political freedom, independence, were no doubt essential, but they were steps only in the right direction; without social freedom and a socialistic structure of society and the state, neither the country nor the individual could develop much".[1]

In his presidential address to the annual Congress session in December 1929, Nehru declared, "I must frankly confess that I am a socialist and a republican, and no believer in kings and princes, or in the order which produces the modern kings of industry, who have greater power over the lives and fortunes of men than even the kings of old, and whose methods are as predatory as those of the old feudal aristocracy".[2] He did not like everything in the Soviet Union and particularly disliked suppression of all contrary opinion, regimentation and violence, but then remembered that the capitalist world also was not free from violence. He was impressed by the reports of progress in Soviet Central Asia. He inclined more and more towards the Soviet Union and its example appeared to him as a bright and heartening phenomenon in a dark and dismal world. He did not treat Marxism as a new religion. In 1933, he said, "What, then, is this Marxism? It is a way of interpreting history and politics and economics and human life and human desires. It is a theory as well as a call to action. It is a philosophy which has something to say about most of the activities of man's life. It is an attempt at reducing human history, past, present and future, to a rigid logical system with something of the inevitability of fate or *kismet* about it."[3]

Nehru disliked fascism and was attracted towards communism. He declared that there was no middle road between fascism and communism and people had to choose between some form of the one or the other. He did not think that the basic ideology of communism and its scientific interpretation of history were sound. In 1935, he said, "I am very far from being a communist. My roots are still perhaps partly in the nineteenth century, and I have been too much influenced by the humanist liberal tradition to get out of it completely. This bourgeois background follows me about and is naturally a source of irritation to many communists".[4] He welcomed the formation of socialist groups in the Congress. In 1936, he declared, "I am convinced that the only key to the solution of the world's problem and of India's problem lies in socialism, and when I use this word I do so not in a vague humanitarian way but in the scientific, economic sense. Socialism is, however, something even more than an economic doctrine, it is a philosophy of life and as such also it appeals to me. I see no way of ending the poverty, the vast unemployment, the degradation and the subjection of the Indian people except through socialism".[5]

Nehru was convinced that India would have to think of its own path to socialism. He imagined that every country would fashion it after its own way and fit in with its national genius. He would not like India to immediately adopt the Soviet model. He declared, "I do not want India to be drilled and forced into a certain position, because the costs of such drilling are too great; it is not worthwhile; it is not desirable from many points of view".[6] In 1936, he said, "Gandhi has played a revolutionary role in India of the greatest importance because he knew how to make the most of the objective conditions and could reach the heart of the masses; while groups with a more advanced ideology functioned largely in the air because they did not fit in with those conditions and could therefore not evoke any substantial response from the masses".[7] He looked upon socialism as an extension of democracy. He remarked that liberty and democracy have no meaning without equality, and equality cannot be established so long as the principal instruments of production are privately owned. Though he considered class struggle inherent in the capitalist system, he had hopes from the non-violent method of struggle in dealing with that problem.

Nehru stresses the importance of human beings having greater and more living contacts with the land and nature. He also lays stress on the value of the ethical approach to life. He said, "I have been attracted by Gandhiji's stress on right means and I think one of his greatest contributions to our public life has been this emphasis".[8] He emphasises that Gandhiji initially opposed the big machine. Later Gandhiji accepted the use of big machines. Nehru draws attention to Gandhiji's emphasis on economic equality.

Between 1927 and 1947, whenever Nehru stressed the efficacy of socialism for solving India's ills, he at the same time stressed the importance of maintaining unity in Congress ranks. He became a link between two generations of Congress leadership and acquired a unique position of importance, equally indispensable to both the conservative old guard or right wing of the Congress and the socialist radicals inside that organisation. He also served as a link between the Congress leadership on the one hand and peasant, trade union and youth leadership on the other. In 1942, he was definitely not in favour of a resort to civil disobedience in support of Gandhiji's call to the British to Quit India immediately. He treated Gandhiji's leadership of the nationalist movement as indispensable and irreplaceable. Gandhi developed a great fascination for Nehru almost from the very start of their relationship, and was highly impressed by the latter's capacity for sacrifice and hard work, his courage and dynamism and his strong appeal to the youth and the intelligentsia. He believed that the Congress needed both the old leaders and the new socialist group. He looked upon the Congress as a united front against imperialism. He did not like the tendency on the part of the old leaders to treat it as a sectarian organisation and run it strictly according to their wishes. He did not also like the attitude of the socialists and other leftists who tended to function like an aggressive opposition group within the Congress.[9]

The National Planning Committee, set up in 1938 at the instance of the Congress, with Nehru as its chairman, contained a wide variety of persons with different backgrounds and views, but that did not dishearten Nehru. His own belief was that real planning was hardly possible under the ordinary structure of society and would inevitably involve the creation of a socialist society. In 1939, he said, "Obviously, constituted as we are, and constituted as the planning committee is, we can hardly begin tackling the question on a socialist basis. We have to accept to a large extent the present structure, at any rate, as a jumping-off ground. At the same time, we must aim at something different, though that need not be, so far as the committee is concerned. . . . If we start with the dictum that only under socialism there can be planning, we frighten people and irritate the ignorant. If, on the other hand, we think in terms of planning apart from socialism and thus inevitably arrive at some form of socialism, that is a logical process which will convert many who are weary of words and slogans".[10]

Nehru showed quite a good grasp of the nature of the communal problem in India in some of his important writings. He pointed out that it would be patently wrong to assert that the Hindu-Muslim problem in India was created by the British Government though at the same time he drew attention to the continuous British efforts to keep that problem alive and to discourage all moves for rapprochement between the two communities. There was some talk of a coalition between the Congress and the Muslim League, particularly in U.P. but this failed to materialise. According to him, the talk of Muslims as a group who might come to an understanding with Hindus as a group represented a medieval mentality which had no place in the modern world. The problems of poverty, unemployment and national freedom were common to all whether they were Hindus, Muslims, Sikhs or Christians.

Nehru did not adopt a firm stand against partition and within a short time of the adoption of the demand by the Muslim League (1940) got it openly affirmed by the Congress that if the majority of people in any part of India became determined upon cessation, that would be conceded without any struggle. He was party to the Working Committee's resolution, adopted in March 1947 without any consultation with Gandhiji, demanding a partition of the Punjab into Muslim and non-Muslim majority provinces. In his discussions with Mountbatten Nehru never put forward any argument against partition at any stage and showed his willingness to accept partition right from the beginning. Perhaps Nehru had by then realised that it was too late to prevent partition. He realised that the principle of provincial option if applied not merely to the areas which were being demanded by the Muslim League for Pakistan, but to the whole of India, might encourage separatist tendencies in India in the long run as well as immediately create difficulties in integrating with the Indian Union the areas ruled by the Indian princes. He wrote to Mountbatten, "The relatively simple proposals that we had previously discussed now appeared, in the garb that H.M.G. had provided for them, in an entirely new context which gave them an ominous meaning. The whole approach was completely different from what ours had been and the picture of India that emerged frightened me. In fact much that we had done so far was undermined and the Cabinet Mission's scheme and subsequent developments were set aside, and an entirely new picture presented—a picture of fragmentation and conflict and disorder, and, unhappily also, of a worsening of relations between India and Britain".[11]

Nehru always attached the highest importance to the likely impact on the unity of the country and on its democratic political structure. In his mind the great value of the Congress lay in the fact that it was the most effective instrument for maintaining political unity in the country. It became his major preoccupation to maintain unity in the Congress. He worked for sixteen to eighteen hours a day and tired himself out attending to things which might have been better left to subordinates, political or administrative. But he failed to set up a regular machinery in order to coordinate or supervise the work of the various ministries. Patel maintained his firm grip over the Congress organisation as long as he lived. With his passing away Nehru emerged as the sole repository of supreme power in the Congress and he maintained this position till his death in 1964.

When Nehru made the Congress adopt democratic socialism as its objective at Avadi in 1955, the majority of the Congress leaders kept quiet and did not consider it wise to oppose him. His role in the Congress reveals the continuity of his style of leadership developed during the days of the freedom struggle, with this difference that as Prime Minister he considered it necessary to assert his supremacy. His main preoccupation was not the reorganisation or modernisation of the Congress, but the preservation of unity in its ranks provided, of course, that no one dared challenge his leadership. He did not attach much importance to the re-entry of the Socialists into the Congress or to its reorganisation was not accidental. In 1963-64, he said, "We have set before us certain values which belong to what might broadly be called a national ideology. Within the framework of this ideology there exist, of course, differences—or, rather, shades of differences. One might be more passionately dedicated to socialism than another, but our approach has always been one of synthesis. There cannot be any other approach for a government or a party representing a vast country of such diversities as India. After all, the Congress was and continues to be more of a national movement than a party".[12]

Nehru showed no interest in encouraging the cultivation of a spirit of austerity by those occupying high offices. He was also extremely reluctant to initiate action against those of his political colleagues who were accused of corruption. He himself remained absolutely free from any taint of corruption or greed for money. His vision gave India her five-year plans which laid the foundations of an industrialised economy and brought about a tremendous expansion in transport and communication and in education and health services. Several dams, factories and scientific laboratories established during the Nehru Era stand as vivid memorials to the achievements of the three five-year plans launched during that period. In 1964, he said, "Frankly, I am not. While industrial and agricultural production has increased considerably, though not to the extent we had planned, the tendency has been towards the accumulation of the national wealth with people at the top—that is, the big businessman and the big farmer—and not towards its equitable distribution among the masses of the people. Thus the rich have grown richer. The poor have also gained, but proportionately less, much less, than the wealthier classes. In result, the gap between the haves and the have-nots has widened. To make things more difficult for the poor classes, there is the accumulation of an enormous amount of black money—that is, unaccounted wealth—in private hands by all means of corrupt practices. This creates an intolerable situation, both economically and from the moral point of view".[13]

Nehru was not prepared to envisage a total break with the past in economic organisation. In 1948, he declared, "I will not say that one should never try to start with a clean state. But one has to think of a country and its condition at the time, and see which is the preferable course, involving less danger. It seems to me that in the state of affairs in the world and in India today, any attempt to start with what might be called a clean state, that is to say, a sweeping away of all that we have, would certainly not bring progress nearer, but might delay it tremendously. Far from bringing economic progress, it might put us so far back politically that the economic aspect itself might be lost sight of. We cannot separate these two things. We have gone through big political upheavals and cataclysms, and if in our attempt to get something that we like and to go forward a step in one direction, we lose a few steps in another, then on balance we have lost, not gained".[14]

Nehru knew that in the prevailing circumstances, the introduction of an entirely new economic system, based on socialism, was not possible through the instrumentality of the Congress and without upsetting the democratic political system. In 1957, he said, "You accuse me of limiting myself to being merely the Congress Party leader. It is difficult for me to judge myself or my activities. Perhaps you are right to some extent, but I do not myself understand what people mean by saying that I should leave party and become. what is called, a national leader. Does that not ultimately mean starting a new party and be limited by that? We have had many great men in the past, who, rebelling against the caste system or something else, ended merely starting a new *sampradaya*. To the multitude of our gods and goddesses and of our sects, they added a few more. Jayaprakash Narayan has frequently summoned me to this national leadership, that is, to get together men of goodwill from all groups and parties and march ahead".[15] In January 1957, he expressed his opinions on the danger to Parliamentary democracy in India. He said, "Jayaprakashji says it would be good for the Congress to be defeated. . . . The issue is what is good for the country, not what is good for the Congress. . . . Suppose in Parliament, instead of the strong Congress Party, we had a dozen or twenty small groups with nobody in a majority. What would happen? There would be no stable government, and each little group would intrigue with the other. There would be offers of ministerships for people who gave up a party to join another".[16]

Nehru's leadership as India's Prime Minister was very much a continuation of his leadership of the nationalist movement. There is no doubt that the style of his leadership as Prime Minister contributed significantly to the strengthening of the foundations of national unity, secularism and democracy. He launched the country on the path of planned development. In 1960, he said, "I have believed in socialism for the past fifty years and, until somebody convinces me to the contrary, I shall continue to believe in and work for socialism. I am not at all embarrassed about being a socialist or our objectives being socialist. That should be the ideal of every sensible nation or society or individual".[17] He was clear in his mind that India must chart out her own, distinct path of development without trying to copy either a capitalist or a communist model. He said, "The problems which India faces are to some extent common to other countries, but we have new problems for which there are no parallels or historical precedents elsewhere. What has happened in the past in the industrially advanced countries has little bearing on us today. As a matter of fact, the countries that are advanced today were economically better off than India today, in terms of per capita income, before their industrialisation began. Western economics, therefore, though helpful, have little bearing on our present-day problems".[18]

Nehru firmly believed that violence would not solve any problem. In 1958, he said "Violence cannot possibly lead today to a solution of any major problem because violence has become much too terrible and destructive. The moral approach to the question has now been powerfully reinforced by the practical aspect. If the society which we aim at cannot be brought about by big-scale violence, will small-scale violence help? Surely not, partly because it produces an atmosphere of conflict and of disruption. . . . In India, any appeal to violence is particularly dangerous because of its inherent disruptive character."[19] He was a firm believer in individual liberty and took pains to emphasise again and again that nothing should be done to impart it in the name of socialism. Socialism must aim at creating a new type of individual. He said, "The touchstone, therefore, should be how far any political or social theory enables the individual to rise above his petty self and thus think in terms of the good of all. The law of life should not be competition or acquisitiveness but cooperation, the good of each contributing to the good of all. In such a society the emphasis will be on duties, not on rights; the rights will follow the performance of the duties. We have to give a new direction to education and evolve a new type of humanity".[20]

The All-India Congress Committee at its meeting in Delhi in 1947 declared, "Political independence having been achieved the Congress must address itself to the next great task, namely, the establishment of real democracy in the country and a society based on social justice and equality. Such a society must provide every man and woman with equality of opportunity and freedom to work for the unfettered development of his or her personality".[21] The Congress committed to work for Democratic Socialism. He said, "The Congress is working for a revolution in the economic and social relationships in Indian society. The revolution is to be brought about through radical changes in the attitudes and outlook of the people as well as the institutions through which they have to function. The object is to attain an economy of abundance in the country by the fullest and the most effective use of human and material resources so that the well-being of every individual can be assured. Everyone should have equal opportunity and a just share in the fruits of progress. Privileges, disparities and exploitation should be eliminated".[22]

Nehru took great interest and played a major role in the framing of India's Constitution. Nehru and Patel constituted the focus of power in the Constituent Assembly and chaired most of its important committees. He took deep interest also in the practical aspects of governance dealt with by the Constitution and was the chairman not merely of the Union Constitution Committee but also of the Union Powers Committee and the State Committee. In 1947, he said, "We will not recognise any independence for any state in India. Further any recognition of such independence by any foreign power, whichever it may be and wherever it may be, will be considered an unfriendly act. . . . There is a certain inherent paramountcy in the Government of India which cannot lapse—an inherent paramountcy in the dominant State in India which must remain because of the very reasons of geography, history, defence etc., which gave rise to it when the British became the dominant power in India".[23] He attached great importance to the debates in Parliament and never missed any important debate. He was indeed most regular in attending the sessions of Parliament, listened carefully to the comments of the members, particularly of those belonging to the opposition, and suitably replied to them. He always saw to it that elections were held as freely and fairly as possible and sought to establish the most healthy traditions in this field.

In Nehru's vision democracy implied equal rights for men and women. In 1955, he said, "You cannot have a democracy if you cut off a large chunk of democracy, fifty per cent of the people, and put them in a class apart in regard to social privileges and the like".[24] He stood firm as a rock in his determination to see to it that all religious minorities got a fair deal in India regardless of the division of the country or the fate of minorities in Pakistan. The Indian Constitution provides for equal rights for all the citizens of India regardless of their religion and all persons are given full freedom to profess, practise and propagate whichever religion they like. He always endeavoured to see to it that minorities in India did not suffer any discrimination at the hands of the state. A major component of his legacy to India, consists of the foundations of her economic development on modern lines laid down under his leadership. It would be wrong to conclude that Nehru attached an undue importance to heavy industries and did not realise the value of small-scale industries. In 1952, he said, "I think the argument one often hears about big industry versus cottage and village industry is misconceived. I have no doubt that we cannot raise the people's level of existence without the development of major industries in this country; in fact, I will go further and say that we cannot even remain a free country then. Certain things, like adequate defence, are essential to freedom and those cannot be had unless we develop industry in a major way. But we must always remember that the development of heavy industry does not by itself solve the problem of millions in this country. We have to develop the village and cottage industry in a big way, at the same time making sure that in trying to develop industry, big and small, we do not forget the human factor."[25]

Nehru did not underestimate the importance of agricultural development. In 1952, he said, "There is much talk of industrialisation. . . . We certainly attach importance to industry; but in the present context we attach far greater importance to agriculture and food and matters pertaining to agriculture. If our agricultural foundation is not strong then the industry we seek to build will not have a strong basis either. Apart from that the situation in the country today is such that, if our food front cracks up, everything else will crack up, too. Therefore, we dare not weaken our food front".[26] All the basic industries developed during his era were placed in the public sector. He did not look upon mixed economy as something permanent or sacrosanct. He looked forward to the steady growth of the public sector and the ultimate fading away of the private sector from the industrial field. The private sector has become today the dominant sector of the economy. He made a major contribution to the economic development by setting up the Planning Commission and making economic planning an integral part of our democratic political system.

The development of modern science in India is another field in which Nehru played a key role. It was his interest in this field which was primarily responsible for the establishment of about thirty research laboratories all over India and of the five Indian Institutes of Technology at different centres. If India today is one of the leading countries in this field, it is largely because of the leadership provided by Nehru. His faith in science as one of the main instruments for building India's future comes out forcefully in his observations. He said, "It is science alone that can solve the problem of hunger and poverty, of insanitation and illiteracy, of superstition and deadening custom and tradition, of vast resources running to waste, of a rich country inhabited by starving people. Who indeed can afford to ignore science today? At every turn we have to seek its aid. The future belongs to science and to those who make friends with science".[27] He never let an opportunity go by without stressing the need for the development of the spiritual side of man. He was firmly convinced that the two must walk together if human beings were to be enabled to lead a life of peace and happiness. He stressed the need for ethical and spiritual solutions to the problems of modern life.

In 1960, Nehru declared, "The emphasis on ethical and spiritual solutions is not unconscious. It is deliberate, quite deliberate. There are good reasons for it. First of all, apart from material development that is imperative, I believe that the human mind is hungry for something deeper in terms of moral and spiritual development, without which all the material advance may not be worth while".[28] He went on emphasising that while modernising our society and giving up outdated customs and traditions we must remain proud of our ancient heritage and not become rootless. There is enough evidence to show that he continued to emphasise the value of the Indian people remaining attached to their ancient heritage even while making advances in science and technology and modernising their society. In 1959, he said, "We must look to the future and work for it purposely and with vigour, at the same time we must keep our past inheritance and derive sustenance from it. Change is essential, but continuity is also necessary. The future has to be built on the foundations laid in the past and the present. To deny the past and break with it completely is to uproot ourselves and sapless, dry up".[29]

In foreign policy the nature of Nehru's leadership was very much conditioned by the evolution of his thinking during the pre-independence period. His foreign policy cannot be properly understood without understanding its historical background. He firmly believed that India must follow its own course in world affairs and not allow itself to be used by any other country. In 1947, he said, "We wish for peace. We do not want to fight any nation if we can help it. The only possible real objective that we, in common with other nations, can have is the objective of cooperating in building up some kind of world structure, call it One World, call it what you like. . . . If we think of that structure and our cooperation with other countries in achieving it, where does the question come of our being tied up with this group of nations or that group? Indeed, the more groups and blocks are formed, the weaker will that great structure become."[30] The policy of non-alignment embodied the heritage of the long Indian struggle for freedom and was not something contrived in haste on the morrow of independence because of India's military weakness or its being new in the field of diplomacy. He laid so much emphasis upon non-alignment primarily because joining any bloc would have meant the curtailment of India's capacity to work effectively for the causes she held dear at the world stage.

Striving for world peace was surely the most characteristic feature of non-alignment as conceived of by Nehru. He treated every major international crisis as a call to action. In 1961, he said, "Non-aligned has a negative meaning. But if we give it a positive connotation it means nations which object to lining up for war purposes, to military blocs, to military alliances and the like. We keep away from such an approach and we want to throw our weight in favour of peace. In effect, therefore, when there is a crisis involving the possibility of war, the very fact that we are unaligned should stir us to feel that more than ever it is up to us to do whatever we can to prevent such a calamity coming down upon us".[31] The foundation of his foreign policy comes out clearly on 7 September, 1946. He said, "We are of Asia and the peoples of Asia are nearer and closer to us than others. India is so situated that she is the pivot of Western, Southern and South-East Asia. In the past her culture flowed to all these countries and they came to her in many ways. Those contacts are being renewed and the future is bound to see a closer union between India and South-East Asia on the one side, and Afghanistan, Iran and the Arab world on the another. To the furtherance of that close association of free countries we must devote ourselves."[32]

Nehru paid due regard to India's own interests and indeed worked for them before taking up anything else. In 1947, he remarked, "whatever policy we may lay down, the art of conducting the foreign affairs of a country lies in finding out what is most advantageous to the country. We may talk about international goodwill and mean what we say. We may talk about peace and freedom and earnestly mean what we say. But in the ultimate analysis, a government functions for the good of the country it governs and no government dare do anything which in the short or long run is manifestly to the disadvantage of that country. Therefore, whether a country is imperialistic or socialist or communist, its foreign minister thinks primarily of the interests of that country".[33]

Nehru was really trying to stress that a foreign policy based on the pursuit of peace should be considered to be in the interest of every nation and not be taken as tantamount to a disregard of national interest.

Nehru realised that if a country's foreign policy has to be effective, it must be based on a national consensus and not become a divisive element in the body-politic. Non-alignment seemed to him ideally suited to build up such a consensus. In 1949, he said, "Any attempt on our part to go too far in one direction would create difficulties in our own country. It would be resented and we would produce conflicts in our own country which would not be helpful to us or to any other country".[34] Again, he said, "Every country's foreign policy, first of all is concerned with its own security and with protecting its own progress. Security can be obtained in many ways. The normal idea is that security is protected by armies. That is only partly true; it is equally true that security is protected by policies".[35]

Nehru relied to a considerable extent on the world balance of power for maintaining India's security. In 1955, he said, "As things are today, we have reached a certain balance—it may be a very unstable balance but it is still some kind of balance—when any kind of major aggression is likely to lead to a world war. That itself is a restraining factor".[36] He did not put too much reliance on the balance of power for the maintenance of world peace. He felt that constant effort was necessary to see not only that the root causes of conflict, such as imperialism and racialism were removed, but also that any crisis situation emerging as a result of the clash between the two superpowers was defused as early as possible and not allowed to escalate into a world war. His diplomacy of peace-making had its own distinctive style based on a mixture of strong yet restrained declaratory statements on the one hand and quiet mediatory efforts on the other.

Nehru's personality and his mastery of words, flowing from deeply felt emotions as well as from an understanding of the historical forces operating in the post-War world, were equally responsible for the impact they made on people's mind in far-flung countries. In 1947, he said, "Far too long have we of Asia been petitioners in Western courts and chancelleries. That story must now belong to the past. We propose to stand on our own legs and to cooperate with all others who are prepared to cooperate with us".[37] At the Asian-African Conference at Bandung in 1955, he remarked, "Of course, Europe and Asia and America are all dependent on one another. It is not right to think in terms of isolation in this modern world which is moving towards the ideal of One World.

Nevertheless, European or some other great countries, whatever the political persuasion may be, have got into the habit of thinking that their quarrels are the world's quarrels and that, therefore, the world must submit to them. I do not follow that reasoning. I do not want anybody to quarrel in Europe, Asia or America, but if the others quarrel, why should I quarrel and why should I be dragged in their quarrel and wars".[38]

Nehru was often misunderstood, both at home and abroad, and accused of partisanship by one group or another, but that did not deter him, and he continued his quest for the right solution unmindful of criticisms. In 1952, he said, "The world is in a ferment of passion and prejudice and I am certain it will do little good to join the crowd of excited people who are shouting at the top of their voices. That will only make things worse".[39] Non-alignment with power blocs, active pursuit of peace and freedom, opposition to imperialism and racialism, interest in developing close relationship with Asian countries, deep concern with the plight of the people of Africa were the fundamentals of his foreign policy. The blend of firmness and flexibility in his foreign policy is also to be noticed in his changing relationship with the great powers within the framework of non-alignment.

Nehru was noted for his modern, scientific outlook and wanted to make India a fully modernised country in every sense of the term through large scale industrialisation and extensive use of science and technology. He adhered to the ideology of democratic socialism and believed that this provided the ideal framework for the building up of a just as well as a free society. He played a notable role in the struggle for Indian freedom and was second to none in his capacity for suffering and sacrifice for that cause.

REFERENCES

1. Jawaharlal Nehru. *An Autobiography*. p. 166.
2. S. Gopal. *Selected Works of Jawaharlal Nehru*. p. 192.
3. Jawaharlal Nehru. *Glimpses of World History*. pp. 562-563.
4. Jawaharlal Nehru. *An Autobiography*. p. 591.
5. S. Gopal. *Selected Works of Jawaharlal Nehru*. pp. 180-181.
6. *Ibid.*. p. 110.
7. *Ibid.*. p. 76.
8. Jawaharlal Nehru. *The Discovery of India*. p. 58.
9. K.S. Bharathi. *Gandhi and Nehru*. pp. 117-118.
10. Nehru to K.T. Shah. 13-5-1939.

11. Nehru to Mountbatten. 11-5-1947.
12. R.K. Karanjia. *The Philosophy of Mr. Nehru.* p. 138.
13. *Ibid.*, pp. 153-154.
14. *Jawaharlal Nehru's Speeches*, I, p. 123.
15. Hiren Mukerji. *The Gentle Colossus*. pp. 138-139.
16. *Jawaharlal Nehru's Speeches*, III. pp. 153-154.
17. R.K. Karanjia, *The Mind of Mr. Nehru*, p. 57.
18. *Jawaharlal Nehru's Speeches*, IV, p. 123.
19. *Ibid.*, p. 118.
20. *Ibid.*, p. 119.
21. Indian National Congress, *Resolutions on Economic Policy, Programme and Allied Matters, 1924-1969*, p. 18.
22. *Ibid.*, p. 146.
23. S.C. Kashyap. *Jawaharlal Nehru and the Constitution*. p. 95.
24. *Jawaharlal Nehru's Speeches*, III p. 451.
25. *Ibid.*, II, p. 94.
26. *Ibid.*, p. 99.
27. *Science Reporter*, July-August 1974.
28. R.K. Karanjia. *The Mind of Mr. Nehru*, p. 32.
29. Jawaharlal Nehru, *India Today and Tomorrow*, p.
30. Jawaharlal Nehru, *India's Foreign Policy*. p. 11.
31. *Jawaharlal Nehru, Speeches*, IV, p. 361.
32. Jawaharlal Nehru, *India's Foreign Policy*, p. 3.
33. *Ibid.*, p. 28.
34. *Ibid.*, p. 47.
35. *Ibid.*, p. 79.
36. *Ibid.*, p. 134
37. *Ibid.*, p. 251
38. *Ibid.*, p. 271
39. *Ibid.*, p. 58.

3

ON SOCIALISM

Nehru has been variously described, during his life and after his death, as a communist revolutionary, a Fabian socialist, a bourgeois democrat or a humanist visionary. In the early thirties, he was regarded by the then rulers as an irreconcilable, who aimed to introduce the Soviet pattern in India, much more dangerous than the other Congress leaders and best put out of mischief by being kept in gaol. According to Bertrand Russel, socialism, like everything else that is vital, is rather a tendency than a strictly definable body of doctrines. Nehru professed socialism and often equated socialism to the Communist ideal, which he accepted. His socialism cannot be questioned merely because, unburdened by Marxist dogmas, he either anticipated some of the objections subsequently raised, or readily adopted his views to the developments which took place after the war, that is immediately before or in the years after India attained independence.

The principle of dialectical materialism explained the growth of societies in the historical process, the contradictions in form of conflict of classes which they give rise to and the resultant changes in the structure of societies. The present capitalist form of society is itself a result of such conflict which emerged in the earlier feudal society, which yielded place to mercantile domination and, later, with the industrial revolution and accumulation of capital, to the capitalists. The recognition of class conflict as an essential feature of socialist thought distinguishes socialism from the widely accepted modern concept of nationalism. The common denominator of socialist thought can be reduced to three basic principles: (1) recognition of the fact that class conflicts exist in non-socialist societies; (2) acceptance of change of property relations; in particular, state ownership of the means of production, as a condition precedent to the resolution of the class conflict; (3) creation of a classless society where class conflict does not exist, or even if it does, is not of significance, and where the state instead of being the instrument of domination by one class can intervene impartially and effectively for all sections of the community.

It was Nehru who in the late twenties and during the thirties of this century popularised the concept of socialism when few in India had given any thought to it. He was less a product of his environment than one who influenced and shaped them. His family heritage was enlarged by his national heritage even while he was a university undergraduate. Later, it was enlarged further by a worldview in which he fitted the national aspirations of his country. He was a Hindu and a Brahmin by birth, and though he was no believer in orthodox Hinduism he adhered to most of the Hindu forms and customs. He spent the first sixteen years of his life in the atmosphere of composite culture, good living secularism. He took part in games and in social life too, and there are letters recounting with clear joy and amusement his experiences of social evenings at school. Even in his school days he showed considerable interest in politics. His letters to his father also contained references to political events in India.

Nehru spent two years in London. During this two years he led the life of an English gentleman. His outlook on life at the time was a vague kind of cyrenaicism. He said, "Not having the religious temper and disliking the repressions of religions, it was natural for me to seek some other standard—I enjoyed life and I refused to see why I should consider it a thing of sin. At the same time risk and adventure fascinated me— Indian politics in 1907 and 1908 were in a state of upheaval and I wanted to play a brave part in them, and this was not likely to lead to a soft life".[2] When he returned to India in 1912 he was a cultured, sensitive human being with wide interests and highly receptive to ideas, from whichever sources they came. His logical mind was not attracted by religious mysticism and even less by dogmas and rituals. Socialist ideas of the Fabian variety had come to him specially during his two years stay in London.

Politics attracted Nehru. The moderate politics which dominated the Congress then did not appeal to him. He said, "Politics, which to me meant aggressive nationalist activity against foreign rule, offered no scope for this".[3] He was moved by the eloquent speeches of Sarojini Naidu. He does not suggest the socialist remedy of socialising the means of production to usher in a classless society. Events soon dragged him into active politics. The biggest single event which overcame his doubts and hesitations was the coming of Gandhiji. In Allahabad he came in touch with the peasant masses. He said, "In 1920 I was totally ignorant of labour conditions in factories or fields, and my political outlook was entirely bourgeois. I knew, of course, that there was terrible poverty and misery, and I felt the first aim of a politically free India must be to tackle the problem of poverty. But political freedom, with the inevitable dominance of the middle class, seemed to me the obvious first step".[4]

In the early twenties Nehru was fully involved in the Gandhian movement. The programme of non-cooperation which Gandhiji had initiated had answered Nehru's keen desire for action. He remarked, "What I admired was the moral and ethical side of our movement and of *satyagraha.* I did not give an absolute allegiance to the doctrine of non-violence or accept it for ever, but it attracted me more and more. . . . The spiritualisation of politics, using the word not in its narrow religious sense, seemed to me a fine idea. A worthy aim should have worthy means leading up to it. That seemed not only a good ethical doctrine, but sound, practical politics, for means that are not good often defeat the end in view and raise new problems and difficulties".[5] He regarded British imperialism as an evil and wanted India to sever all connections with it. He stood for complete independence.

Nehru's experience of rural poverty in his province as well as the happenings in Russia had rekindled his interest in socialism, but it was his latent boyhood nationalism which now found an outlet in the Gandhian programme that occupied his mind fully. In 1921, he said, "As the achievement of *swaraj* is only possible if people of all professions live in union and as the tenants and zamindars can be truly happy only when independence is so achieved, so this Conference expresses its desire that the tenants and zamindars live in harmony through mutual goodwill and sympathy, and insists that although the recent Rent Act has made their position worse, still they should patiently bear all trouble, pay their rents and keep the welfare of the country in view".[6] He accepted the Congress view that the interests of the peasants and the landless should be subordinated to the needs of the national struggle which required that the social *status quo* should be maintained to make joint effort possible.

Gandhian non-violence and its insistence on right means to achieve worthy objectives came to Nehru as the answer he had sought for the problem of his country where the liberal values had been violated by ruthless imperialism. He had his differences with Gandhiji right from the start. In 1923, he said, "Bolshevism and Fascism are waves of the

West today. They are really alike and represent different phases of insensate violence and intolerance. The choice for us is between Lenin and Mussolini, on the one side, and Gandhi, on the other. Can there be any doubt as to who represents the soul of India today?"[7] He was attracted by the social objectives of socialism.

The Brussels Congress proved to be a milestone in the development of Nehru's political thought, notably his espousal of socialism and a broad international outlook. He had no doubts about the objective of the Brussels Congress. In 1927, he said, "The whole basis of the League is that imperialism and capitalism go hand in hand and back each other, and neither of them will disappear till both are put down. An endeavour is therefore made to join the forces against imperialism and capitalism and by their coordination strengthen the two".[8] He agreed with the socialist theory of the State in its fundamentals, but he had some hesitation about the strategy proposed to be adopted by the League. He said, "the principal objects of the Congress, as disclosed in the agenda, were to bring about cooperation between such movements of various countries. This presupposes that there is a great deal in common not only between the national movements but also between them and the workers' struggle for emancipation. The former appears obvious enough. . . . The second supposition however raises deeper problems. Are the interests of the workers in other countries the same as our national interest?".[9]

Nehru's statement to the Press on the eve of the Brussels Congress was indeed a forth right attack on Imperialism, as also was his speech at the Congress. His attraction to Marxism was perhaps the most striking feature of his role at the Brussels Congress. He was undoubtedly even at this stage intensely anti-imperialist but his anti-imperialism was born of his nationalism, not of Marxism or even of his attraction to Marxism. He had indeed a certain attraction for Marxism. He declared, "As between the Labour worlds of the Second International and the Third International, my sympathies were with the latter. The whole record of the Second International from the War onwards filled me with distaste, and we in India had sufficient personal experience of the methods of one of its strongest supporters—the British Labour Party. So I turned inevitably with goodwill towards Communism, for whatever else its faults, it was at least not hypocritical, not imperialistic. It was not a doctrinal adherence, as I did not know much about the fine points of Communism, my acquaintance being limited at the time to its broad features".[10] His participation in the Brussels Congress undoubtedly marked an important stage in the development of his thoughts.

Nehru strongly recommended that the Indian National Congress should become an associate member of the League. In 1927, he said, "the League is a new organisation and has all manner of elements in it. It is not possible to say how it will develop, or whether it will develop at all. The Congress can hardly exercise any control over its policy or its funds from such distance. . . . Nevertheless I am clearly of opinion that the Congress should take any risk, if risk there is, and associate itself with the League".[11] His thoughts at this stage were still in a state of evolution. They had not yet arrived at the socialist conclusions. His predominant emotion was nationalism. He was keen that the poorer sections, the peasants and the workers, should be fully involved in the national struggle. He said, "This will happen only when the masses, who are the people who suffer most, become conscious of the situation. They appear to be near such an awakening. Peasant associations and industrial trade unions are gradually being formed and when they have gained strength, they will to a great extent control the political movement".[12]

Nehru returned to India full of energy and vitality, and plunged straight into Congress politics at the Madras session of Indian National Congress. He said, "The sense of inner conflict and frustration that had oppressed me so often previously was, for the time being, absent. My outlook was wider, and nationalism by itself seemed to me definitely a narrow and insufficient creed. Political freedom, independence, were no doubt essential, but they were steps only in the right direction; without social freedom and a socialistic structure of society and the State, neither the country nor the individual could develop much".[13] He had always been in favour of complete independence for India. At the Subjects Committee meeting in Madras, he said, "this Congress declares the goal of the Indian people to be independence with full control over the defence forces of the country, the financial and economic policy and relations with foreign countries. The Congress demands that this right of the people of India should be forthwith recognised and given effect to, in particular by complete withdrawal of the alien army of occupation".[14]

Nehru had no difficulty in getting the Congress to accept his recommendation that the Indian Congress should become an associate member of the League against Imperialism. He reentered politics not only with enthusiasm but indeed with a changed outlook. At the Republican Conference in Madras, he remarked, "It was important for them to form some kind of organisation which would keep the National Congress up to the mark and also prepare the country for a republican ideal. The world had adopted republicanism".[15] On 5 January 1928 in *Young India*, Gandhi wrote, "though I was not able to attend any of the Committee meetings, I could not fail to perceive that irresponsible talk and work were the order of the day. Indiscipline was not a rare feature. Resolutions involving great consequences were sprung upon the Subjects Committee and readily accepted by that august body without much thought or discussion".[16]

On 11 January 1928, Nehru wrote a letter to Gandhiji. He wrote, "Reading many of your articles in *Young India*—your Autobiography etc.—I have felt how different my ideas were from yours. You have stated somewhere that India has nothing to learn from the West and that she had reached a pinnacle of wisdom in the past. I entirely disagree with this viewpoint and I neither think that the so-called *Ram Raj* was very good in the past, nor do I want it back. I think the Western or rather industrial civilisation is bound to conquer India, may be with many changes and adaptations, but nonetheless in the main based on industrialism. You have criticised strongly the many obvious defects of industrialism and hardly paid any attention to its merits. . . . I believe that you have stated that in your opinion there is no necessary conflict between capital and labour. I think under the capitalist system the conflict is unavoidable".[17]

Nehru travelled a great deal all over the country during 1928-1930. He said, "Everywhere I spoke on political independence and social freedom and made the former a step towards the attainment of the latter. I wanted to spread the ideology of socialism especially among Congress workers and the intelligentsia, for these people, who were the backbone of the national movement, thought largely in terms of the narrowest nationalism".[18]

The main features of the socialist thinking Nehru had adopted are worthy of note. He was strongly in favour of complete independence, and was opposed to Dominion Status or to any other arrangement within the British Empire. On 11 April 1928, he said, "Many of us who denounce British imperialism in India do not realise that it is not a phenomenon peculiar to the British race or to India, or that it is the necessary consequence of industrial development on capitalist lines. For capitalism necessarily leads to exploitation of one man by another. Therefore, we are opposed to this imperialism and exploitation. We must also be opposed to capitalism as a system, and to the domination of one country over another. The only alternative that is offered to us is some form of socialism, that is, the state-ownership of the means of production and distribution".[19] On 12 December 1928, he said, You have probably often condemned British imperialism because you suffer under it. But have you thought it is but a manifestation of a world phenomenon? And this world phenomenon is the direct outcome of a system of society which prevails in the greater part of the world today and is called capitalism. Your immediate problem and mine is to gain political freedom for our country, but this is only part of the problem facing us".[20]

Nehru recognised the existence in capitalist societies not only of conflict of class interests but also of class consciousness as a determining factor in attitudes of different classes. On 30 November 1928, he said, "We are often accused of preaching class war and of widening the distance between the classes. The distance is wide enough, thanks to capitalism, and nothing can beat the record of capitalism in that respect. . . . Is it the socialist or the communist who separates the classes and preaches discontent or the capitalist and imperialist who by his policy and methods has reduced the great majority of mankind into wage-slaves who are worse even in many ways than the slaves of old. The class war is none of our creation. . . . The class war has existed and exists today".[21] On 29 May 1928, he declared, "the non-cooperation movement was started, about eight years ago, by the upper intelligentsia in India who controlled it. There was a mass element in that movement and certainly it made the Congress a strong body. It was powerfully affected by the mass element, but most of its leaders became frightened and agitated. . . . Later on, when non-cooperation movement gradually developed, the control of leaders became less and less and they suspected the masses from the beginning. Then the liberal leaders kept themselves aloof from it. Thus while the masses became more and more aggressive the leaders were less and less aggressive in their turn. This divorce between the masses and the leaders brought about the downfall of that movement".[22]

Nehru's statements and speeches during the period make it clear that while he did not at any stage accept the methods of communism, he accepted its aims and objectives, and regarded the capitalist system. based on the private profit motive and on competition, as inequitable. He wanted the system to be replaced by a socialist system based on cooperation, and on freedom of each individual to develop according to his capacity. He never accepted Marxism as a dogmas or a holy doctrine. He recognised nationalism as a sentiment which evoked strong emotional response in the country. He did not accept the criticism that socialism with its emphasis on class conflict would raise discordant voices and thus retard the national movement. He said, "the voice that claims it (freedom) must be the voice of revolt, the dull and threatening roar from a hundred thousand and a million throats, not the sweetly modulated tone of an accomplished debater. . . . The voice of the masses will only be raised if you put before them an ideal and a programme which affects them and improves their economic condition, and when raised it will only be followed by action if the end in view is worth the struggle and sacrifice".[23] Freedom to him was indivisible. It had a social as much as a political content. Without the former, the latter had no meaning.

Nehru organised an Independence for India League as a pressure group within the Congress. He wanted a body of earnest men of deep conviction who have a living faith in some economic programme. In 1929, he said, "The object of the League is to achieve independence for Indian society on a basis of social and economic equality. . . . It means that the League aims at a socialistic, democratic state in which every person has the fullest opportunities of development and the state controls the means of production and distribution".[24]

Nehru was specially interested in the peasantry and made no secret of his view that the community of zamindars was superfluous. In 1930, he remarked, "the economic programme for the nation should lay down that the principal industries of the country are owned and controlled by the state, and the land is owned, as far as possible, by the peasant who works on it".[25] In a letter addressed to the Secretaries to the League on 30 January, 1930, he wrote, "I am afraid you have not the least notions of conditions in India and yet you do not hesitate to lay down the law for us".[26]

The Karachi resolution was the first concrete instance where the economic thinking of Nehru was accepted, though only partially, by the movement. He continued to lead the movement till his arrest at the end of December 1931. Some of his pronouncements were indeed radical, for he talked of war with government and made no secret of his personal view that zamindari as a system should go. The U.P. agrarian movement provides an instance of the influence that he had on the Congress in spite of his differences with Gandhiji and the majority of the Congress leadership.

In order to achieve the goal of classless society Nehru emphasised the need of total transformation of social life through democratic methods. He was of the opinion that the process of rich becoming richer and poor becoming poorer has to be stopped by planned method so that the poor can rise above their condition whenever opportunity arised. But in his political philosophy there was only revolutionary thinking instead of revolutionary action. This was the basic difference between him and the other socialists.

Nehru was greatly impressed by the efforts of the Soviet Union to bring about total change in the social life by planned methods after the revolution. Even then he could not accept the practical form of communism. In fact there is self-contradiction in communism implied in denial of individual freedom, indifference towards humanitarianism, contempt for moral and spiritual aspect of life. Communism has deprived human experience of values and ideals. Due to its relation with violence communism has encouraged bad tendency in man. Classless society is a noble ideal but violent methods cannot be supported for its realisation. He considered violence as wholly unscientific, irrational and uncivilised methodology. He said, "Socialism ultimately is not only a way of life but also a scientific point of view about social and economic problems. It we implement socialism in a backward and undeveloped country it will not eliminate backwardness together. In fact we will be left with only a poor and backward society".

Nehru stressed the need of social and economic changes for evolving a socialistic society. In the third decade of this century he said, "I have gradually accepted the point of view of scientific socialism and now I can claim myself as a socialist in the real sense of the term". In 1936, he said, "Political freedom is implied in socialism because without it there cannot be social and economic freedom". After 1934 he continuously talked of socialism as the only remedy of poverty, unemployment and other social problems. On 19 May, 1936, he said, "We have to construct a new social system in which all are assured of equal opportunities for development, in which there will be no exploitation, in which there will not only be political democracy, but also economic democracy in the form of economic equality".

Nehru attached great importance to the views of Jayaprakash Narayan, Acharya Narendra Dev and Acharya Kripalani. In 1938 he declared, "I am certainly a socialist. I have faith in the socialist thinking and methodology. I am not a communist because I am against the tendency of communists to consider the communist doctrine as sacred. I also do not like somebody telling me how I should think and how

I should act". It was this attitude which led him to invite the socialists in 1953 for cooperation. For nearly seventeen years after independence he remained solely responsible for determining social, political and economic policies of the country. During this period he always talked about the scientific socialism and worked for construction of really socialist society. For him, socialism was a philosophy of life. He laid emphasis on four important conditions for solving the problems of India through socialism, raising of the standard of life of general masses, providing them better means of life, providing them opportunities for physical, cultural and spiritual development, and ending of economic disparity gradually by non-violent means.[27]

On analysis of Nehru's socialism we notice a few very important features which kept him away from other socialists of the country. First and foremost is that he wanted to bring about social and economic change through gradual and non-violent methods. Due to religious and cultural heritage of India combined with a long period of foreign domination the process of gradual change remained stationary to a great extent. As a result of it economic disparity continued even with best intentions of the government. He laid the basis of planned development according to the Russian pattern but even after two Five Year Plans during his life time the basic problems of poverty and unemployment remain unsolved. At the time of achieving independence India was divided into castes and sub-castes with complete control of capitalism over the economic system of the country. For social and economic transformation of the country it was necessary to end both of these systems. The Constitution made provision for ending caste system through law but nothing was done to destroy capitalism. As against this the capitalist class took under its influence the country's politics using all possible means. In this way it became nearly impossible to bring about economic change according to the socialist principles. Thus he could not put into practice his socialist philosophy. Ultimately he had to accept private sector and public sector working together for socialist pattern of society.

Before independence Nehru talked about nationalisation of industries and socialisation of the entire economic system. After assuming power he removed this from the list of priorities. Socialism is a practical philosophy and for achieving this ideal what is required is extreme reformative measures. Karl Marx said very clearly that the capitalist class would not voluntarily withdraw its influence over the society and all the privileges of enjoyment. This is perfectly right and has been proved during all these years after independence. The socialist leaders had only one complaint against Nehru that he attached too much importance to slow and gradual change and did not take effective steps to improve the lot of the poor people. For giving more importance to socialist thinking against socialist practice he could not realise the ideals of socialism in spite of being a great socialist thinker.

Congress accepted the ideal of a socialistic pattern of society at the Avadi session of the Congress in 1955 under Nehru's inspiration. It connoted social ownership or control of the principal means of production, acceleration of national production and equitable distribution of the wealth of the nation. His own concept of a socialist pattern of society visualised social and economic equality, removal of disparities and the opportunity of everyone for work and employment so as to ensure a reasonable standard of life. He did not however, subscribe to the thesis that socialism may be termed as equivalent to accentuation of production only through heavy industries in the public sector. In the true Gandhian background he recognised the place of rural industries and *khadi* in his scheme of economic reconstruction. In 1938, he made it clear that planning included development of the cottage and small-scale industries to provide employment opportunities in labour-intensive Indian economy, where the small-scale industries have the vast potentialities of providing basic commodities of mass consumption besides the employment opportunities. Similarly his concept of socialism laid full stress on agrarian reconstruction in India through the implementation of land reforms. In the matter of planned development he envisaged a key role for the public sector in the field of basic and heavy industries, heavy chemicals, power generation and transport and communication, etc. In the field of consumer goods industries he would concede an adequate role for the private sector. Thus he attempted to put socialism as a concrete objective of the social and economic reconstruction through the concept of a 'mixed economy' within the framework of a parliamentary democracy.[28]

Nehru had no hesitation to call himself a socialist and he had his own conceptions of socialism. In 1929, he declared, "We must realise that the philosophy of socialism has gradually permeated the entire structure of society the world over, and almost the only points in dispute are the peace and the methods of advance to its full realisation. India will have to go that way, too, if she seeks to end her poverty and inequality though she may evolve her own methods and may adopt to the genius of her race. Our economic programme must be based on a human outlook and must not sacrifice man to money. If an industry cannot be run without starving its workers, then the industry must close down. If the workers on the land have not enough to eat, than the intermediaries who deprive them of their full share must go". In his *Glimpses of World History*, he remarked, "Socialism is of many kinds. There is general agreement, however, that it aims at the control of the state of the means of production—that is land and mines and factories and like—and the means of distribution like railways, etc. and also banks and similar institutions. The idea is that individuals should not be allowed to exploit any of these methods or institutions, or the labour of others, to their own personal advantage". Today most of these are privately owned and exploited, with the result that some people prosper and grow rich, while society as a whole suffers greatly and the masses remain poor. The abolition of the zamindari system and consequent land reforms, the nationalisation of major financial institutions and means of transportation, etc. all had their roots in his firm belief in socialism within a democratic framework relevant to the Indian situation, especially in the post-independence India.

Nehru had his disagreement with those Indian socialists of the contemporary era who borrowed the socialist ideas from Karl Marx and Lenin but he did not realise its implications in the context of the Indian situation. In his Autobiography, he said, "I was by no means a pioneer in the socialist field in India. Indeed I was rather backward and I had only advanced painfully, step by step, where many others had gone ahead blazing trail. The workers trade union movement was, ideologically, definitely socialist, and so were the majority of the youth leagues. A vague confused socialism was already part of the atmosphere of India when I returned from Europe in 1927, and even earlier than that there were many individual socialists. Mostly they thought along utopian lines, but Marxian theory was influencing them increasingly, and a few considered themselves as hundred per cent Marxists. This tendency was strengthened in India, as in Europe and America, by developments in the Soviet Union, and particularly the Five Year Plan".

Nehru was convinced that vast changes that socialism envisages cannot be brought about by the sudden passing of a few laws in the Indian situation. Basic law and power are necessary to give direction of advance to lay the foundation of the structure on which the edifice of a socialist society can be built through the active involvement of the people whose emancipation it seeks to bring about. In 1936, he observed, "I am convinced that the only key to the solution of the world's problems and of India's problems lies in socialism. I see no way of ending the poverty, the vast unemployment, the degradation, and the subjection of the Indian people except through socialism. That involve vast and revolutionary changes in our political and social structure, the ending of vested interests in land and industry as well as the feudal and autocratic Indian state system. That means the ending of private property, except in a restricted sense, and the replacement of the present profit system by a higher ideal of cooperative service".

Nehru had a firm conviction that socialist objectives need not necessarily be achieved through violent revolution and at the cost of individual freedom and liberty. He saw great merit in individual liberty and freedom and to some extent in the institution of private property. In his essay in Unity of India, he remarked, "I do not see why under socialism there should not be a great deal of freedom for the individual; indeed, far greater freedom than the present system gives. He can have freedom of conscience and mind, freedom of enterprise, and even the possession of private property on a restricted scale. Above all, he will have the freedom which comes from economic security, which only a small number of persons possess today".

Nehru's faith in socialism and democracy was demonstrated in his statement in 1939. He said, "I have been and am a convinced socialist and believer in democracy, and have at the same time accepted whole-heartedly the peaceful technique of man. Violent action which Gandhiji had practised so successfully during the past twenty years. I am convinced that strength can only come to us from the masses". As far as India is concerned, he disagreed with the view that class-interests should be subordinated and, if necessary, be sacrificed to national interests until freedom was won.

Democratic socialism was the brain child of Nehru. To achieve it, he launched economic planning in India. The seeds of present day policies of mixed economy, were sown during his tenure as Prime Minister. He gave an economic system to India which is being followed even today. He was very much ahead of his time, but unfortunately, he did not live long to see the implementation of his ideas. The seeds of the economic fruits which India is repaying today were sown by none else than Nehru. He was convinced that socialism was bound to come, and the only dispute could be about the method of achieving it. However, he conceded that India could evolve her own method and adapt the ideal of socialism to the genius of her race. Though he spoke of socialism and of a classless society, he was no communist. He did not believe in the inevitability of violence for transforming the socio-economic order.[29]

Nehru attacked those who criticised socialism as being unIndian or not being spiritual enough. It seemed amazing to him that while millions starved and suffered, these critics ignored their lot, talked of vague metaphysical ideas and shirked the problems of today in futile debate about yesterday; that when thoughtful people all over the world were considering how to lessen human misery, Indians, who needed betterment most, talked complacently of what their ancestors did thousands of years ago and allowed their countrymen to continue to grovel on the ground. He felt that opposition to socialism sprang really from attachment to vested interests, and, sometimes, from ignorance.

Nehru's socialism had an agrarian bias. He realised that in an agricultural country like India, development of peasant organisations was essential. He said that the Indian communists had associated mostly with the industrial workers in big towns and they had little knowledge of, or contact with, the peasants, but the Congress workers, he hoped, would spread into the countryside so that the Congress would develop into a vast peasant organisation. He argued that socialism is not spreading out of poverty. There must be wealth and production.

No account of Nehru's socialism would be complete without a brief reference to his ideas on the problem of land reform. He has pointed out that the present land system in India is of relatively recent origin. This, according to him, is but another undesirable product of imperialism. The British introduced different forms of land ownership in different regions. This was a deliberate policy of the British by which a new class of big land-owners was created whose interests depended upon the continuance of British rule. Despite its origin, the problem of landlordism is a most serious menace. Nehru realised its seriousness at a very early date and held that for the Congress the agrarian question was the dominating social issues. He contends that for the solution of this problem the withdrawal of British imperialism was the prime need. He has been convinced that the size of land-holdings should be limited by law to what is ordinarily sufficient for a family to cultivate. Abolition of big estates is for him a prerequisite of increasing production and general progress.

The conflict between the dynamic forces moving towards economic equality and the static rights of the individual is, according to Nehru, the greatest menance to the prosperity of the country. His approach to the problems of economy is a pragmatic one rather than theoretical as his earlier doctrinaire philosophy tended to be. He asserts not only that the achievement of a socialist state by democratic process is possible but also that this is the only way to build it up on firm foundations. The goal of socialism is for him the gradual evolution of a classless and casteless society bereft of the profit motive and individual greed. His socialism is neither dreamy nor fanciful but calls for the desired social regeneration.

Nehru's contribution in giving practical shape to socialism however lay in the fact that he tried in his own way to clothe the concept with an aura of mass appeal. He succeeded to a great extent in making socialism a practical slogan to which the nation as a whole responded enthusiastically. Even before India became independent, he had visualised the necessity of planning. No wonder, therefore, that the Planning Commission under his direct supervision and guidance launched the country on the path of planned growth in every sphere. His faith in democratic methods was in itself a contribution to socialism, since it helped in creating a stable polity wherein it was possible to channelise the energy of the nation towards the programme of national reconstruction. In his own life-time he emphasised the importance of science and technology and laid the firm basis for their growth by establishing a number of national laboratories which have been doing useful work. His love for socialism was responsible for the expansion of heavy industries in the public sector. Vast irrigation schemes were part of his attempts to modernise agriculture.

According to Nehru, socialism had no meaning for the people, if they could not participate actively in planning their own future. Panchayat Raj was for Nehru an essential step in the direction of modernisation, without which socialism could remain only an ivory tower concept in India. His greatest contribution to the cause of socialism in India was his constant and continuous endeavours in the cause of world peace. His deep involvement in the problems of the world, seemingly even at the expense of national problems, was deliberate because he had realised that peace in the world was essential if the under-developed and developing nations were to make progress and provide the minimum necessities of life to their citizens.[30]

During the freedom movement, Nehru's socialistic ideas influenced the youth and the intelligentsia of the country. After independence, it was thought that the cause of socialism was safe with Nehru at the helm of affairs. But the socialists outside the Congress party were greatly disappointed and were very vocal in their criticism against Nehru who, according to them betrayed the cause of socialism. He was concerned with evolving a set of principles and ideas to achieve a socialist reconstruction of society with democratic means rather than with a violent revolution. His conviction was that socialism without democracy would mean tyranny in the Indian context. Before and after independence, his main concern was to push his socialist ideas to the Congressmen. He said, "I wanted to spread the ideology of socialism especially among Congress workers and the intelligentsia for these people, who were the backbone of the national movement, thought largely in terms of the narrowest nationalism".[31]

Nehru made efforts to lay down the foundations of an industrial society by starting steel plants, heavy electrical and tool factories. His abolition of landlordism and feudal princely states, and his revolutionising of the economic structure by emphasising the role of heavy industries was a great contribution. His concept of "Mixed Economy" encouraged and strengthened capitalism in spite of the Public Sector. The monopoly power of the capitalists increased during the seventeen years of his socialism. He did not bring any radical change in property relationships. He was so obsessed with increase in production that he could not realise that the benefits of economic development would go more to the already well-off sections of society. Under the leadership of Nehru, the Congress was making commitment to socialist programmes and policies. His belief was that the Congress party could commit itself to socialism, it would be very difficult either for his successors or the party to give up its belief in socialism and economic planning. He was trying to make socialism a national goal, and for this he was educating the masses and converting his party men. He thought that such efforts should lead India towards socialism. His faith was that progress towards the goal, through his methods, might be slow but it would be steady and firm. He was convinced that if the majority of the people actively supported the cause of socialism, it had great prospects in India.[32]

Nehru was confident that the new revolutionary mass line as was emerging in the fight for national liberation against the big imperialist powers was powerful enough to win freedom and defend it and to build socialism provided they stood together and followed the path of non-alignment. Socialism is the logical outcome of this revolutionary mass line that has brought the masses to the forefront of the national life as the freedom-fighters and as the new nation-builders. Apart from its other virtues, non-alignment is a means of preserving their spirit of self-reliance and self-sacrifice and of doing things by themselves without learning on others. National freedom and socialism require the entire masses of the nation to pass through such an ordeal of hard struggle, self-sacrifice and suffering. These are not things to be given as a gift by other powerful nations, nor things to be borrowed or copied, but are things to be grown in the soil of the country by sacrifice and hard struggle through trials and errors and experiences, according as the conditions of the country necessitate. As life cannot be borrowed or taken as a gift, so also is freedom or socialism which is new way of life. Nehru's line of socialism stemmed from his broad humanitarian world outlook to liberate mankind, and derived strength and foresight from his scientific concept of socialism. He saw socialism coming as the next inevitable stage in the course of historical development, to save society from the conflict created by capitalism with modern science, blocking its advancement and creative use and the path of social progress, and also to end international conflicts.

Nehru was a nationalist with democratic convictions gradually moving towards socialism. That was the real order of priorities in his own personal picture of the Indian scene whatever might have been the rhetoric of earlier years. He did not see any alternative to the democratic process in a multi-lingual, large, diffused society like India where there had to be a conscious effort by the rulers and the elite, all the time, to bring back into mainstream unassimilated groups in the outer fringes. At the same time democracy was the only method by which justice, at least in the future, would be assured to the large majority of the population who had not immediately benefited by independence and who continued to remain in conditions of deprivation. A democratic constitution based on adult franchise and with an assured, periodic opportunity for the people to register their views was, thus, inevitable. At the same time Nehru knew that the introduction of socialism in its original sense of state ownership of means of production and community control of all utilities would have been unrealistic in a nation which had more pressing pre-occupations in caste, communalism and poverty. This is the reason why socialism was not mentioned in the original constitution but came later into it in the attenuated term "socialistic" denoting democracy with social justice, or socialist planning based on democratic premises.

Nehru did not set himself out to be a prophet for the world, either for the future or even more modestly his own generation. He saw himself in human terms as a leader trying to impose some sort of pattern on a wild chaotic society whose gifted people were trying to live down centuries of exploitation and create a new world, not necessarily brave or powerful but basically decent. He carefully distinguished himself from Gandhi whom he regarded as a prophet, an irresistible personal force in history, a rare individual who comes once or twice only in a millennium and who is not concerned with the practical problems and the details and the compromises which worry the political leader.[33] Democracy without socialism leads inevitably to intolerable deprivation and social injustice.

To Nehru, democracy and socialism had to go together; they did not in a properly planned system neutralise each other, but provided mutually reinforcing elements. He fully realised that his method look longer than adopting short-cuts to socialism by imposition, but on the other hand the results would be more enduring. This sensitiveness to democracy was in his mind intertwined with Gandhiji's insistence on the precedence of means over ends. He said that we would have to understand that our background is in many ways peculiar particularly the Gandhian background. His belief in socialism and democracy was integrally related to his awareness of the need for a peaceful international environment. He educated the people to think in forward-looking terms in building a new society and inculcated democratic and socialist values. He attached great importance to the individual in the social process. He believed in a humane and equitable social order. The supreme objective was to achieve higher standards of living for the common man. Socialism to him was not a dogma but a set of principles to be adapted to the Indian context.

Impressed by the achievement of socialist planning Nehru accepted socialism as the guiding philosophy of India because of poverty in India as well as the developments in Socialism all over the world. He was also aware that socialism is devoid of democratic values and for the proper development of human personality and the growth of just society democratic values are indispensable. So, he combined the socialist philosophy with the democratic values of capitalist society which is popularly described as the democratic socialism.

Nehru was a firm believer in socialism but he had his love for democracy also. Socialism demanded the centralisation of all the means of production and distribution and vesting the ownership only in the hands of the state to wage the marathon war against poverty and the people have to sacrifice all non-economic values for waging the war successfully. Examples are Soviet Union and China. Nehru definitely did not want this type of war against poverty. He chose the socialistic pattern which will have the economic ideals of socialism and democratic values of capitalism. The combination of the ideals of socialistic and capitalistic economy resulted in the mixed economy.

Nehru's democratic socialism rejects violence and relies on persuasion and education; it recognises freedom, liberty and dignity of human beings as socialism is combined with democracy; it aims at the provision for everybody of a national minimum in terms of housing, clothing, food, education and health, at the reduction of inequalities and checking of monopolies, at the provision of equal opportunities to all without any distinction of caste, creed and religion, at the maximisation of production in order to banish poverty and unemployment, at the social ownership and control of basic and heavy industries and a dominant role of public sector. It also recognises the vital role of private sector and the significance of cottage and small scale industries; it does not advocate the nationalisation of everything; it is not merely an economic concept, but a philosophy of life.

Nehru's inability to usher in socialism may be attributed, in the first instance to the fact that his concept of socialism itself was very vague and ill-defined. His attitude with regard to socialism wavered and fluctuated. He lacked the political will for building up socialism in India. Another factor which hampered his attempt to bring socialism in India was the nature of state in which he had to operate after independence. The Constitution-makers were hesitant to use the word socialism in Constitution. He wishes to usher socialism in the country without bringing about radical changes in the socio-economic structure. He failed to establish the requisite administrative apparatus for realising the goal of socialism. He adopted the administrative organisation that had been inherited from the British. He adopted a capitalist model of development in India during his Prime Ministership. His concept of mixed economy promoted capitalism in India. He did not build a political party which could become an useful instrument in bringing about socialism. He had to face strong opposition of the rightist forces in the Congress Party during the fifties. He gradually developed an unfortunate tendency to identify unconsciously the fortunes of the Congress Party with interests of India as a whole. The unchallenged rule of the Congress Party at the centre as well as in the states also paradoxically proved a hurdle in his way so far as building of socialism was concerned. The weakness of the leftist forces in India also played a role in reducing the pressure for socialism in his mind.[34]

Nehru was a great nationalist. But he was against the tendency of isolation. Peaceful co-existence for him was the practical form of non-alignment. He was of the opinion that millions of people living in non-aligned countries would work as a great moral force in holding the big powers from entering into conflict. He considered Panchasheel as the only guarantee for the future of mankind.

REFERENCES

1. R.C. Dutt, *Socialism of Jawaharlal Nehru*, p. 10.
2. Jawaharlal Nehru, *Autobiography*, p. 26.
3. *Ibid.*, p. 30.
4. *Ibid.*, p. 49.
5. *Ibid.*, p. 73.
6. S. Gopal, *Jawaharlal Nehru*, Vol. I, p. 61.
7. Jawaharlal Nehru, *Selected Works*, Vol. 2, p. 210.
8. *Ibid.*, p. 287.
9. *Indian Quarterly Register*, Vol. II, 1927, pp.154-155.
10. Jawaharlal Nehru, *Autobiography*, p. 166.
11. Jawaharlal Nehru, *Selected Works*, Vol. 2, p. 332.
12. *Ibid.*, p. 348.
13. Jawaharlal Nehru, *Autobiography*, p. 166.
14. Jawaharlal Nehru, *Selected Works*, Vol. 3, pp. 3-4.
15. *Ibid.*, pp. 7-8.
16. *Collected Works of Mahatma Gandhi*, Vol. XXXV, pp. 437-38.
17. Jawaharlal Nehru, *Selected Works*, Vol. 3, pp. 14-15.
18. Jawaharlal Nehru, *Autobiography*, p. 182.
19. Dorothy Norman, *Nehru—The First Sixty Years*, pp. 156-157.
20. Jawaharlal Nehru, *Selected Works*, Vol. 3, p. 204.
21. *Indian Quarterly Register*, 1929, II, p. 426.
22. Jawaharlal Nehru, *Selected Works*, Vol. 3, p. 243.
23. Bombay Presidency *Youth Conference*, 12-12-1928, p. 209.
24. Jawaharlal Nehru. *Selected Works*, Vol. 3, p. 287.
25. *Ibid.*, Vol. 4, pp. 255-256.
26. *Ibid.*, p. 237.
27. K.S. Bharathi, *Gandhi and Nehru*, pp. 96-97.
28. *Ibid.*, pp. 98-100.
29. *Ibid.*, pp. 101-103.
30. S. B. Gupta, *Nehru's Socialism*, p. 278.
31. Jawaharlal Nehru, *Autobiography*. p. 182.
32. C.P. Bhambhri. *Nehru, Democracy and Socialism*, pp. 286-287.
33. A.K. Damodaran. *Jawaharlal Nehru and Democratic Socialism*, pp. 293-298.
34. Ranbir Singh. *Nehru and Socialism*, pp. 254-259.

4

ON FREEDOM

Personal freedom generally includes freedom of speech and expression, freedom to form associations and freedom of press etc. Nehru was convinced that law and order are the last refuge of the reactionary, of the tyrant and of him who has power and refuses to part with it. He emphasised that the government which has to make excessive use of coercive apparatus and has to depend on criminal law and emergency powers forfeits its right to exist. In 1936, he said, "A government that has to rely on the Criminal Law Amendment Act and similar laws, that suppress the press and literature, that bans hundreds of organisations, that keeps people in prison without trial, and that does so many other things that are happening in India today is a government that has ceased to have even a shadow of a justification for its existence."[1] Suppression of freedom and personal liberty leads to intellectual and moral degeneration of the people and makes the government autocratic.

Nehru wanted Indian policy to be based upon the respect for individual freedom and dignity. To him, individual was always an end and never a means. In 1931, he said, "Every citizen of India has the right of free expression of opinion, the right of free association and combination, and the right to assemble peacefully and without arms, for a purpose not opposed to law and morality. . . . All citizens are equal before the law, irrespective of religion, caste, creed or sex."[2] His opinion about personal freedom began to change as soon as he became the Prime Minister. In 1948, he remarked, "I have stood for the freedom of the individual and the group, and nothing pains me so much as that condition should arise in this country when Civil Liberties should be limited. . . . It pains me and hurts me that the very thing, I condemned in the past should be indulged in by our governments."[3] Again in 1956, he said, "I believe that ultimately it is the individual that counts . . . no individual is trivial. Every individual has an importance and he should be given full opportunities to develop. . . . They should be common to everybody."[4]

Nehru was not a protagonist of unrestricted freedom. An individual had no absolute freedom to act as he liked. He said, "In a democratic society, the concept of individual freedom has to be balanced with social freedom and the relations of the individual with the social group. The individual must not infringe on the freedom of other individuals."[5] To him, state was an agency for protecting the right of freedom of the individual. He said,"Social life necessitates some form of government, and the men so placed in authority must curb and prevent all individuals or group tendencies which are inherently selfish and likely to injure society".[6] He firmly believed that freedom did not mean indulging in wrong methods and inciting violence for some selfish ends. He remarks, "It is the paramount duty of government to give security to the people and to prevent the normal life of the community from being interfered with by such methods of violence. No government and no social life would be possible if these methods were tolerated."[7]

A balance must be struck between the security of the state and the freedom of the individual. If the individual is to be protected by law, society is also to be protected against the selfish and predatory individual. Nehru's idea of the welfare state rested on the good of the individual. In his thinking freedom of expression, speech, writing and press occupies a key place. A believer in democracy should believe in this fundamental freedom. Suppression of thought stunts the growth of the whole social group. In 1936, he said, "I claim the right of free criticism of public policies and I gladly acknowledge this right in others who may be opposed to my views. Only thus can we have glimpses of the truth and hammer out a right policy."[8] He always tried to encourage honest criticism of public policies and government. He remarked, "I welcome criticism and I welcome you pointing out all our failings. . . . I think it is good for an individual and for a nation always to try to find where it is going wrong and to correct itself. Never be afraid of criticism".[9]

Freedom of the press was not merely a slogan but an essential attribute of the democratic process, said Nehru. He preferred to have a completely free press with all the dangers involved in the wrong use of that freedom than a suppressed or regulated press. The freedom of the press did not mean the lack of suppression by governmental authority alone, but it essentially meant the editorial freedom which was being endangered by the wealth owners and proprietors of newspapers. He maintained that freedom of expression and press had to be considered in relation to the life and the circumstances existing in a country at a particular time. He said, "Conditions differ and exactly the same principles may apply but the application of the principle may differ. . . . I don't think that exactly the same type and extent of freedom can be applied in all circumstances at all times".[10]

The state reserves its basic right to protect itself against internal disorder and violence. Nehru remarked, "While we want freedom, freedom of the press or freedom of speech or freedom of anything, we have to remember that the nation must be free and the country must be free".[11] He curtailed civil liberty only when war forced him to do so. In Rajya Sabha, he said, "In India we have to face the new situation against a background of democratic freedom. To some extent these freedoms have to be limited. There is the Defence of India Ordinance which is not functioning wholly as it is meant to. We do not like to enforce even the Defence of India Ordinance unless we are forced to do it. At the moment we are inhibited in acting, even in regard to stopping a man from writing and publishing something".[12] He held that every state must have the right of police power for in the name of freedom and sanctity of constitution no state could afford to risk its safety and existence. The rule of law and independent judiciary were considered by him as essential guarantees for the personal freedom of the individual.

Nehru developed an aversion towards religion from the very beginning. He declared, "I am not wedded to any dogma or religion; but I do believe whether one calls it religion or not—in the innate spirituality of human beings. I do believe in the innate dignity of the individual".[13] In 1949, he said, "I cannot speak about religion because that word has so many meanings in different minds and the kind of religion we see about us in every country is more of a husk and a ritual than anything having a real content".[14] He felt completely frustrated with the practice of religion. According to him religion is narrow and intolerant of other opinions and ideas, it is self-centred and egoistic. He said, "I am not a religious man, dogmas do not appeal to me".[15] Religion gave a permanent and an honoured place to poverty and misery in this world. He said, "The very ideals of liberty and equality were opposed to the authoritarian outlook of the Church and society".[16] He fully supported the mental and spiritual development of man.

Nehru was sceptical about the existence of God and held that after all God is a creation of man's mind. He condemned the religious man as selfish because he is concerned far more with his own salvation than with the good of society. In 1954, he said, "I wish to declare with all earnestness that I do not want any religious ceremonies performed for me after my death. I do not believe in any such ceremonies and to submit to them would be hypocrisy and an attempt to delude ourselves and others".[17] His religion was the service of India. He said, "I am trying to serve my country. If service to my country is religion, I am religious. If it is not, I am not".[18] His association with Gandhiji failed to instil into him any attraction for orthodox religion, but it left an indelible stamp on him, as far as moral values were concerned. He opined, "Some faith seems necessary in things of the spirit which are beyond the scope of our physical world, some reliance on moral, spiritual and idealistic conceptions, or else we have no anchorage, no objectives or purpose in life".[19]

Nehru was very much influenced by scientific outlook. He said, "Religion, as I saw it practised, and accepted even by thinking minds, did not attract me. It seemed to be closely associated with superstitious practices and dogmatic beliefs, and behind it lay a method of approach to life's problems which was certainly not that of science".[20] He looked at science as the only way to pull India out of the old grooves of thought and put her on the track to modernity. His scientific temper and agnosticism could not but make him a non-religious man. To quote Vincent Sheean, "I do not discover, in his printed work or in any talk I have had with him during the past twelve years, one vestige of the religiosity which otherwise obsesses Hindu culture. This is truly extraordinary in India".[21]

For Nehru, secularism was not only a political doctrine, but a social one of revolutionary character which embraced all religions and all communities in India. He said, "a purely secular philosophy of life may be considered enough. . . . And yet that secular philosophy itself must have some background, some objective other than merely material well-being. It must essentially have spiritual values and certain standards of behaviour".[22] The first feature of secularism, according to him, was the granting of equal states to all religions in India. He said, "I find it difficult to appreciate why political or economic rights should depend on the members of a religious group or community. I can fully understand the right to freedom in religion".[23] He always believed in multi-religious India. He declared, "India is a common home to all those who live here to whatever religion they may belong . . . they have equal rights and obligations. Ours is a composite nation".[24] Again in 1951, he said, "As India is a secular state, every citizen has the same duties, rights, privileges and obligations as any other. He has full freedom to profess and practise his religion".[25]

The second feature of secularism, according to Nehru, was neutrality of the state in matters of religion. He said, "I am convinced that the future Government of free India must be secular, in the sense that Government will not associate itself directly with any religious faith".[26] He always condemned in strong words any talk of Hindu Raj or Muslim Raj. He believed in people's raj and for that state was expected to follow a policy of co-existence as far as various religions were concerned. The third feature of secularism, according to him, was an attitude of mind. It meant a mental attitude on the part of various communities. He said, "From the religious point of view, it is the dominant community and it is its responsibility not to use its position in any way which might prejudice our secular ideal".[27] Again he declared, "Hindus must always remember that the interest and the well-being of the minorities are their sacred trust. If they fail in their trust, then they injure not only the country, but themselves".[28] He cautioned and appealed both to the majority and minority communities not to adopt attitudes which are wrong and opposed to what we stand for.

The fourth feature of secularism, according to Nehru, was that all areas of social life in India must be secularised. He said, "Hinduism and Islam, quite apart from their purely religious teachings, lay down social codes and rules about marriage, inheritance, civil and criminal law, political organisation, and indeed almost everything else. In other words, they lay down a complete structure for society and try to perpetuate this by giving it religious sanction and authority. Hinduism has gone farthest in this respect by its rigid system of caste".[29] He tried to evolve a uniform civil code for the whole of Indian people irrespective of the distinctions of religion and caste by introducing many measures of social legislation. He regarded secularism as the essential feature of a modern democratic society. His secularism was a practical necessity in India as a solution to the problem of religious diversity which was a challenge to her unity, harmony and social stability.[30]

Nehru's ideas regarding social freedom revolves around two issues. Firstly the abolition of the caste system and secondly social freedom and social justice to scheduled castes and scheduled tribes. To him, individual was a nucleus around whom all activities and all human relations revolved. He maintained that real progress will come only when opportunity is given to the individual to develop. He said, "The foundations of progressive and stable society and state were harmony, unity and social equality".[31] So every one must have the opportunity to develop to the best of his or her ability. He said, "We are all equal partners in the freedom that we have won. Every one of our three or four hundred million people must have an equal right to the opportunities and blessings that free India has to offer".[32]

Nehru felt that caste system was most dangerous in the interest of social justice in India. The caste system in the Indian social order was essentially a group system based on service and functions. On the basis of membership of a particular caste, the place of an individual was determined in society and it was difficult for him to free himself of these group loyalties and obligations. He said, "It held Indian life together for thousands of years, and it could only do so, not by preventing change or growth, but by allowing this to take place".[33] He found that with the growth of rigidity in the caste system, rigidity of mind also increased and the creative energy of the race faded away. He believed that the caste system itself contained seeds of its decay for it was based on perpetuating inequality and injustice. He said, "In the context of society today, the caste system and much that goes with it are wholly incompatible, reactionary, restrictive and barriers to progress. There can be no equality in status and opportunity within its framework, nor can there be political democracy and much less economic democracy".[34]

Nehru was of the opinion that no sound and stable society could be built-up on the basis of inequality and injustice, or on the exploitation of one class or group by another. He failed to reconcile himself to the continued existence of the caste system and repeatedly appealed for its total abolition. In 1951, he said, "The practice of casteism was retarding the country's progress. We have already suffered heavily due to the caste system. We have therefore to fight this demon and to provide equal opportunities for every citizen of India, irrespective of any caste, creed to make progress".[35] In 1961, he remarked, "Anyhow the caste system . . . did a lot of harm in undermining the older thinking and older ways of life of the Indians. While once they travelled abroad. . . now they were cut off from the world, which was very bad for them".[36] To him, caste was a throwback to some ideas of medievalism and had no meaning in a society which claimed to develop equality.

In the Constituent Assembly Nehru remarked, "It becomes incumbent upon us, not only for humanitarian reasons but from the standpoint of the fulfilment of democracy, to raise up those people who are low down in the social and economic scale and to bring to them every possible opportunity of growth and progress".[37] He tried to eradicate the caste system. He believed that the state, as one of the most basic social institutions must anticipate social needs and act accordingly.

Nehru always emphasised the need for giving special opportunities to the suppressed and oppressed backward classes. He said, "Our social programme must lay down clearly that we cannot tolerate the many disabilities which various classes called the depressed classes suffer from".[38] Again he said, "Special opportunities for educational, economic and cultural growth must be given to backward groups so as to enable them to catch up to those who are ahead of them".[39]

The Advisory Committee on Minorities and Fundamental Rights recommended that some seats in the central and state legislatures should be reserved for some specified minority and socially backward communities. Nehru felt that the idea of reservation of seats was communal in character. Later on, he said,"So far as the government is concerned, it does not wish to have any truck with communalism in any form: all that it wants to do is to help the backward classes as . . . irrespective of what religion or group they belong to, then it is our duty to help them to advance educationally, socially and economically".[40] He was in favour of the removal of all those descriptions and names which ideologically and physically separate the people as the Depressed Classes, the Harijans, the Scheduled Castes, the Scheduled Tribes and so on. His love for mountains brought him in contact with the tribes of Assam in 1937. He said, "No people in India require more helpful sympathy and cooperation from their countrymen than those tribal folk and others who live cut off from us in these areas".[41] He felt that the tribal folk of India should be given due importance and protection.

Nehru held that the tribal people were more educated and disciplined and led a better corporate life than the caste-ridden society that we suffer from. He was not interested in uprooting the tribals from their ways of life without giving them something new to live on. He wished that the government officers who go to work in tribal areas should not keep themselves apart from the life of the tribal people, but should try to understand them and to reach their heart by sharing their life. To him, the government must encourage the development of tribal languages and all the possible facilities should be granted to them. He went to the extent of disfavouring prohibition among the Nagas and other tribes against their will for drink was a part and parcel of their life. He observed that the struggle for freedom in India unleashed a great liberating force but it could not reach these remote tribal areas.[42]

Nehru was convinced that economic freedom was the basis for all other freedoms. To him, economic freedom must be based on equality, well-being of the masses and cooperative spirit. Throughout his political career, he worked for the economic freedom of the peasants and industrial workers. He defined economic freedom as: "First of all, that means working for a certain measure of well-being for all, call it welfare state. Secondly it means working for a certain measure of equality of opportunity in the economic sphere".[43] His ideal of an egalitarian society was a cooperative ideal, a one world ideal, based on social justice and economic equality. In 1955, he said, "I also want a classless society in India and the world. I do not want any privileged classes. I do not want a great deal of inequality among people".[44] He condemned a society where some people live in luxury without doing any work, whilst others work from morning to night with no rest or leisure and yet have not got the barest necessities of life. In 1928, he said, "Our economic programme must aim at the removal of all economic inequalities and an equitable distribution of wealth".[45]

The second basis of economic freedom was well-being of the masses. Nehru believed that the masses were to be given the right to live and to pursue happiness, which economic progress could alone bring. He declared, "I have been driven almost against my will to the conclusion that material well-being is just as important in human life as anything else. High standard of living are important and we must achieve them".[46] He emphasised that no society and no government could afford to ignore the urges of the common people. He described a welfare state thus: "This will mean our deliberately aiming at a new type of society whose chief purpose is the welfare of the people, not only in material living stand aids but also in the things of the spirit".[47]

The third basis of economic freedom was cooperative spirit. A new socio-economic organisation based on equality and freedom should not be guided by the motive of private profit and competitive violence. but by the principle cooperation and service to the community for the common good. A transformation of social outlook and individual motivation was very important. This transformation could be brought about by socialism. He said, "We have to aim deliberately at a social philosophy which seeks a fundamental transformation of this structure, at a society which is not dominated by the urge for private profit and by individual greed . . . we must aim at a classless society based on cooperative effort, with opportunities for all".[48]

Nehru regarded both fascism and communism as totalitarian concepts based on the power of the state and social group. He was totally against fascism. He said, "I dislike fascism intensely and indeed I do not think it is anything more than a crude and brutal effort of the present capitalist order to preserve itself at any cost".[49] Again, he said, "There is no middle road between fascism and communism. One has to choose between the two and I choose the communist ideal. I may not agree with everything that the orthodox communists have done".[50] He disapproved of communism on many grounds. He said, "In spite of its apparent success, it fails, partly because of its rigidity, but even more so, because it ignores certain essential needs of human nature. . . . Its suppression of human freedom brings about powerful reactions. Its contempt for what might be called the moral and spiritual side of life, not only ignores something that is basic in man, but also deprives human behaviour of standards and values. Its unfortunate association with violence encourages a certain evil tendency in human beings".[51]

Nehru did not support the communist ideal fully. In 1955, he said, "We believe in democracy, equality and removal of special privileges and we have set ourselves to the goal of developing a socialistic pattern of society through peaceful methods".[52] Regarding equality in 1933, he said, "Democracy means equality and democracy can only flourish in an equal society".[53] Equality in a democracy does not mean equality of possessing a vote, but economic and social equality. His ideal was social equality in the widest sense and equality of opportunity for everyone. He said, "Every man and woman must have the opportunity to develop to the best of his or her ability. . . . Honour and merit must come from ability and hard work and not because of caste or birth or riches".[54] Political and social freedom and equality must lead to economic freedom and equality. Freedom and poverty are incompatible. He said, "Freedom becomes unimportant where there is absolute poverty. . . . If through poverty and for other reasons you do not have even the capacity to live worthily, all other freedoms do not count".[55]

Nehru realised the chances of conflict between political freedom and economic freedom. He said, "Real freedom ultimately comes from political freedom and economic freedom. . . . But the point is this. There is a conflict between the economic as pest and political freedom

. . . in countries which are under bondage and underdeveloped, where there is starvation and want for millions of people, those people are more interested in a good meal or a certain economic betterment than in some theoretical political freedom".[56] He was very much impressed by both liberal democratic ideas emphasising freedom and socialistic ideas emphasising equality. He remarked, "Political freedom or political equality is the very basis on which you build up other equalities. At the same time political equality may cease to have meaning if there is gross economic inequality".[57] In 1936, he said, "I agree with you also that the political phase comes first; indeed without that phase there is no other phase. It may be accompanied by social changes. . . . Presumably I am perfectly prepared to accept political democracy only in the hope that this will lead to social democracy. Political democracy is only the way to the goal and is not the final objective".[58]

Nehru's concept of freedom is an integrated concept including social, political and economic aspects. He said, "It is impossible to separate the political life of the country from its social and economic life and you cannot cure the social organism by treating one part of it only".[59] He believed that the rivalry between capitalism and democracy was inherent and continuous. He also believed that history provided enough proof of the fact that economic interests shaped the political views of groups and classes. He was firmly convinced that the only way to save human beings from utter degradation was socialism. In 1936, he said, "I am convinced that the only key to the solution of the world's problems and India's problems lies in socialism, and when I use this word I do so not in a vague humanitarian way but in the scientific economic sense. Socialism is, however, something even more than an economic doctrine, it is a philosophy of life and as such also it appeals to me".[60]

Socialism is closely related to the welfare of the society and the well-being of the people. In 1960 Nehru said, "I have believed in socialism for the past fifty years, and until somebody convinces me to the contrary, I shall continue to believe in and work for socialism. . . . That should be the ideal of every sensible nation or society or individual. Modern thinking all over the world is increasingly becoming socialist and only people who have lost touch completely with contemporary trends can think otherwise".[61] In his *Autobiography* he gave the concept of his final society. He said, "Our final aim can only be a classless society with equal economic justice and opportunity for all, a society organised on a planned basis for the raising of mankind to higher material and cultural levels; to a cultivation, unselfishness, the spirit of service, the desire to do right, goodwill and love-ultimately a world order".[62]

For the achievement of economic freedom Nehru accepted Gandhiji's non-violent approach. He said, "I have been and am a convinced socialist and believer in democracy and have at the same time accepted whole-heartedly the peaceful technique of non-violent action, which Gandhiji has practised so successfully during the past twenty years".[63] Though his conception of democracy was not metaphysical, yet it included ethical and moral values. He tried to apply his socialistic ideas to Indian problems as soon as India was free. He realised that the true test of progress and freedom in India lay in the change in the status and conditions of life of the peasant. He urged the Congress to adopt an agrarian programme. In 1936, he said, "The most important and urgent problem of the country is the appalling poverty, unemployment and indebtedness of the peasantry, fundamentally, due to the antiquated and repressive land tenure and revenue system".[64]

In 1952 after seeing the slums Nehru said, "These slums represent the utmost form of human degradation. Those responsible for this state of affairs should be hanged".[65] He stressed the importance of industrial workers in a developing economy and realised that they were the most dynamic factor in our society today. He worked hard for spreading the ideology of socialism in India and urged the Congress to adopt socialistic programmes. He favoured a mixed economy for future India. In February 1950, the National Planning Commission was set up with Nehru as its Chairman. In January 1955, the Indian National Congress at Avadi adopted a resolution moved by him. It said, "Planning should take place with a view to the establishment of a socialistic pattern of society, where the principal means of production are under social ownership or control, production is progressively speeded up and there is equitable distribution of the national wealth".[66]

In 1959, the Indian National Congress at Nagpur adopted a resolution of far-reaching importance regarding cooperatives. It remarked, "The future agrarian pattern should be that of joint cooperative farming in which the land shall be pooled for joint cultivation, the farmers continuing to retain their property rights. . . . As a first step prior to the institution of joint farming service cooperatives should be completed within a period of three years".[67] Nehru believed that one must learn from others wherever one could, but one must also maintain one's own foundations. He said, "We have to understand our problem as it is in India, no doubt learning from what has been done in America, England, Yugoslavia, Russia or China but at the same time bearing in mind that the conditions in India are special and particular. Further, we have also to understand that our background is in many ways peculiar, particularly the Gandhian background".[68]

Nehru was greatly fascinated by the concept of planning as a right approach for economic freedom. He accepted planning not as an end but as a means. For him, democracy and planning were not incompatible. He said, "If anybody is going to tell me that a democratic structure means no planning, I am not prepared to accept that statement".[69] To him, a society based on *laissez faire* was itself unable to provide real freedom to the individual. Democracy and freedom cannot survive for long in midst of want, inequality and economic insecurity. He said, "Planning is essentially a process whereby we stop those cumulative forces at work which make the poor-poorer and start a new series of cumulative forces which make them get over that difficulty".[70]

Nehru held that in a democratic structure nothing could be forced down the throat of the people by compulsion and coercion. He admitted that centralisation has become a technological social necessity of the present age and this leads us to one of the central problems of our civilisation how to combine freedom with planning. Planning is not opposed to the essential freedom of man. He said, "If we adhered to the democratic state structure and encouraged cooperative enterprises, many of the dangers of regimentation and concentration of power might be avoided".[71] For him, the plan was meant to bring about a new social order free from exploitation, poverty, unemployment and injustice. He stressed the need for common welfare of the people. He recognised the important role of plans as a social process. He believed that India which is most vulnerable to narrow tendencies could be united through the introduction of uniform planning.

Nehru did not believe in changing the existing system by violence. He said, "It seems to me that in the state of affairs in the world today and in India, any attempt to start with what might be called a clean state, that is to say, a sweeping away of all that we have, would certainly not bring progress nearer, but might delay it tremendously".[72] Again, he said, "There is a powerful urge for change because of existing economic conditions. The urge comes from the people and not from some people's heads. So there is that pressure which urges on the democratic apparatus to go ahead".[73] He tried to win economic freedom through land reforms, cooperative farming and Community Development Programme. For achieving economic freedom in urban and industrial area he propounded a new idea of socialistic planning based on mixed economy which envisaged division of country's economy in the state owned public sector and the private sector. He realised the importance of cottage industries in bringing about economic freedom for the people of India.

REFERENCES

1. Jawaharlal Nehru, *India and the World*, p. 74.
2. Jawaharlal Nehru, *The Unity of India. 1937-40.*
3. Devas S.. *Nehru: Champion of Peace*, 1960.
4. Mishael Brecher, *Nehru: A Political Biography*, p. 607.
5. *Nehru's Speeches*, Vol. II, p. 499.
6. Jawaharlal Nehru, *An Autobiography*, p. 542.
7. *Constituent Assembly Debates*, Vol. II. pp. 1110-11.
8. Jawaharlal Nehru, *Eighteen Months in India*. p. 20
9. Jawaharlal Nehru, *Independence and After*, p. 181
10. *Nehru's Speeches*, Vol. II, pp. 465-66.
11. *Ibid.*, p. 526.
12. *Ibid.*, p. 109.
13. *The Hindu*, 28 March 1960.
14. Jayaswal, S.R., '*Nehru on Society, Education and Culture*, 1965.
15. Mende, T., *Conversations with Nehru*, p. 144.
16. Jawaharlal Nehru, *Glimpses of World History*, p. 545
17. Norman, D., *Nehru: The First Sixty Years*, Vol. II, p. 574
18. Balakrishnan, V.V., Nehru's Religious Philosophy. *The Sunday Standard*, 25 May 1969.
19. Bright, J.S.. *Selected Writings of Jawaharlal Nehru. 1916-1950.*
20. Jawaharlal Nehru, *The Discovery of India*, p. 26.
21. Sheean, V., Nehru, *The Years of Power*. p. 22.
22. Jawaharlal Nehru, *The Unity of India*, p. 180.
23. Bright, J.S.. *Selected Writings of Jawaharlal Nehru, 1916-1950.*
24. Jawaharlal Nehru, *Independence and After*, p. 30
25. *The Hindu*, 14 July 1951.
26. Bright, J.S., *Before and After Independence*, p. 252.
27. Jawaharlal Nehru, *Letters to the P.C.C. Presidents*. pp. 19-20.
28. *Ibid.*, p. 3.
29. Jawaharlal Nehru, *Glimpses of World History*, p. 762.
30. Saroj Prasad, *Nehru's Concept of Freedom*, p. 193.
31. Bright, J.S. *Before and After Independence*. p. 79.
32. Jawaharlal Nehru, *Independence and After*, p. 28.
33. Jawaharlal Nehru. *Glimpses of World History*, p. 115.
34. Jawaharlal Nehru, *The Discovery of India*, p. 270.
35. Dewas, S., *Nehru: Champion of Peace*, p. 24.
36. *Prime Minister Nehru's Visit to U.S.A.*. John Day and Coy. New York. p. 114.

37. Jawaharlal Nehru. *Independence and After*. p. 50.
38. Bright. J.S.. *Before and After Independence*. p. 124.
39. Jawaharlal Nehru. *The Discovery of India*. p. 554.
40. *Nehru's Speeches*, Vol. II. p. 487.
41. Jawaharlal Nehru. *The Unity of India*. p. 197.
42. Saroj Prasad. *Nehru's Concept of Freedom*. pp. 94-95.
43. *Nehru's Speeches*. Vol. IV, p. 70.
44. *Ibid*.. Vol. III, pp. 136-137.
45. Bright. J.S.. *Before and After Independence*. p. 124.
46. *Nehru's Speeches*. Vol. II, p. 563
47. Jawaharlal Nehru, *Report to All India Congress Committee*. p. 8.
48. *Nehru's Speeches*. Vol. II, p. 93.
49. Jawaharlal Nehru. *Recent Essays and Writings*. p. 126.
50. *Ibid*., p. 126.
51. Nehru and Yudin. *On the Basic Approach*. p. 3.
52. Sharma. J.S., *Jawaharlal Nehru: A Descriptive Biography*, p. 349.
53. Jawaharlal Nehru, *Glimpses of World History*, p. 854.
54. Bright, J.S., *Selected Writings of Jawaharlal Nehru*, p. 59.
55. *Nehru's Speeches*, Vol. IV, p. 182.
56. *Jawaharlal Nehru's Press Conferences*, 1950, p. 126.
57. Cousins, N., *Profiles of Nehru*, pp. 19-20.
58. Jawaharlal Nehru, *A Bunch of Old Letters*. p. 143.
59. Bright. J.S. *Before and After Independence*, pp. 56-57.
60. Jawaharlal Nehru, *India and the World Essays*, p. 82.
61. Karanjia, R.K., *The Mind of Mr. Nehru*, p. 57.
62. Jawaharlal Nehru, *An Autobiography*. pp. 551-52.
63. Jawaharlal Nehru, *The Unity of India*, p. 134.
64. *Ibid*., p. 408.
65. Saxena, R.C., *Labour Problems and Social Welfare*, p. 212.
66. Michael Brecher, *Nehru: A Political Biography*, p. 528.
67. *Democratic Research Service Cooperative Farming*, p. 3.
68. *Nehru's Speeches*, Vol. III, pp. 16-17
69. *Ibid*., p. 70.
70. *Ibid*., Vol. IV. p. 112.
71. Jawaharlal Nehru, *The Discovery of India*. p. 425.
72. Jawaharlal Nehru, *Independence and After*, p. 174.
73. Mende, T.. *Conversations with Nehru*, pp. 97-98.

5

INDIAN NATIONAL CONGRESS

Nehru delivered the Presidential address at the 49th Session of the Indian National Congress held in April 1936 at Lucknow. The Presidential address has been reproduced here as such: After many years I face you again from this tribune, many years of strife and turmoil and common suffering. It is good for us to meet again; it is good for me to see this great host of old comrades and friends, linked together by strong bonds that cannot break, to sense the old brave spirit yet again, to feel your overwhelming kindness and goodwill to one whose greatest privilege it is to have been a comrade and a soldier with all of you in a mighty struggle for freedom. I am heartened and strengthened by you, though even in this great gathering I feel a little lonely. Many a dear comrade and friend has left us, worn out, long before the normal length of our earthly days, by the stress and strain of conflict. One by one they go, leaving a void in our hearts and a dull misery in our minds. They find peace from this turmoil perhaps, and it is well, for they deserved it. They rest after labours.

But what of us who remain behind with a heavier burden to carry? There is no rest for us or for those who languish in prison or in detention camp. We cannot rest, for rest is betrayal of those who have gone and in going handed the torch of freedom to us to keep alight; it is betrayal of the cause we have espoused and the pledge we have taken; it is betrayal of the millions who never rest.

I am aware and I have come back like a child yearning for solace in the bosom of our common mother, India. That solace has come to me in overflowing measure; thousands of hands have been stretched out to me in love and sympathy; millions of silent voices have carried their message of affection to my heart. How can I thank you, men and women of India? How can I express in words feelings that are too deep for utterance?

For many years now I have been a distant looker-on on this Indian scene where once I was an actor, and many a thing has happened that has filled me with distress and anguish. I do not wish to survey this recent past of ours, which must be fresh in your memory, and which has left a sorry trial behind and many knots which are difficult to unravel. But we may not ignore it for out of that past as well as the present, we have to build our future. We have followed high ideals and we have taken pride in the fact that our means are worthy of those ideals. We have been eye witnesses of many a miracle in this old and battered land of ours, and yet our very success has been followed by failure and disillusion. Temporary failure has little significance when the aim is high and the struggle bound to be a long one; it is but the incentive to further effort. Often it teaches us more than a victory easily won and becomes a prelude to a greater success. But we profit by it only if we learn its lesson and search our minds for an explanation of that failure. Only by constant self-questioning individual and nations, can we keep on the right path. An easy and unthinking confidence is almost as bad as a weak submission to helpless dejection. Real failure comes only when we forget our ideals and objectives and principles and begin to wander away from the road which leads to their realisation.

In this crisis of our history, therefore, let us look into ourselves and examine, without pity or prejudice, what we have done and what others have done to us, and seek to find out where we stand today. We dare not delude ourselves or evade real issues for fear of offending others, even though some of these others are comrades whom we respect. That is the way of self-deception which none who seek great and vital changes can follow except at their peril.

Sixteen years ago, under the inspiration of our leader, we took a new and long step converting this Congress from an ineffective body, feebly functioning amongst the upper classes, into a powerful democratic organisation with its roots in the Indian soil and the vast masses who live on it. A handful of our old friends, representing an age and a class which had had its day, left us, fearful of this democratic upsurge, and preferring the shelter and protection of British imperialism to joining hands with the new vital forces which convulsed the country and struggled for freedom. Historically, they lapsed into the past. But we heard the rumbling of those forces and, for the moment, lined up with them and played a not unworthy part in current history. We sensed the new spirit of mass release, of psychological escape from the cramping effects of long subjection; we gloried in the breaking of the mental bonds that encompassed us. And because our minds became free we felt that political freedom could not be far, for it is often harder to break the bonds of the spirit than physical bonds and chains of iron and steel. We represented the Spirit of the Age and were marching step by step with countless others in our country and outside. The exhilaration of being in tune with the masses and with world forces came upon us and the feeling that we were the agents of historic destiny.

We were engrossed in our national struggle and the turn it took bore the powerful impress of our great leader and of our national genius. We were hardly conscious then of what was happening outside. And yet our struggle was but part of a far wider struggle for freedom, and the forces that moved us were moving millions of people all over the world and driving them into action. All Asia was astir from the Mediterranean to the Far East, from the Islamic West to the Buddhist East; Africa responded to the new spirit; Europe, broken up by the war, was struggling to find a new equilibrium. And right across a vast area in Europe and Asia, in the Soviet territories, a new conception of human freedom and social equality fought desperately against a host of enemies. There were great differences in the many aspects of this freedom struggle all over the world and we were misled by them and did not see the common background. Yet if we are to understand these varied phenomena and derive a lesson from them for our own national struggle, we must try to see and understand the whole picture. And if we do so we cannot fail to observe an organic connection between them which endures through changing situations. If once we grasp this organic bond, the world situation becomes easier to understand and our own national problems take their proper places in the wider picture. We realise then that we cannot isolate India or the Indian problem from that of the rest of the world. To do so is to ignore the real forces that are shaping events and to cut ourselves adrift from the vital energy that flows from them. To do so, again, is to fail to understand the significance of our own problems, and if we do not understand this how can we solve them? We are apt to lose ourselves, as we have indeed done, in petty conflicts and minor questions, like the communal problem, and forget the major issues; we are apt to waste our energy in interminable discussions over legal quibbles and constitutional questions.

During the troubled aftermath of the Great War came revolutionary changes in Europe and Asia. There were ups and downs, and sometimes it appeared as if revolutionary urge had exhausted itself and things were settling down. But economic and political conditions were such that there could be no settling down, the existing structure could no longer cope with these new conditions, and all its efforts to do so were vain and fruitless. Everywhere conflicts grew and a great depression overwhelmed the world and there was a progressive deterioration, everywhere except in the wideflung Soviet territories of the USSR, where, in marked contrast with the rest of the world, astonishing progress was made in every direction. Two rival economic and political systems faced each other in the world and, though they tolerated each other for a while, there was an inherent antagonism between them, and they played for mastery on the stage of the world. One of them was the capitalist order which had inevitably developed into vast imperialisms, which, having swallowed the colonial world, were intent on eating each other up. Powerful still and fearful of war, which might endanger their possessions, yet they came into inevitable conflict with each other and prepared feverishly for war. They were quite unable to solve the problems that threatened them and helplessly they submitted to slow decay. The other was the new socialist order of the USSR which went from progress to progress, though often at terrible cost, and where the problems of the capitalist world had ceased to exist.

Capitalism, in its difficulties, took to fascism with all its brutal suppression of what western civilisation had apparently stood for; it became, even in some of its homelands, what its imperialist counterpart had long been in the subject colonial countries. Fascism and imperialism thus stood out as the two faces of the new decaying capitalism, and though they varied in different countries according to national characteristics and economic and political conditions, they represented the same forces of reaction and supported each other, and at the same time came into conflict with each other, for such conflict was inherent in their very nature. Socialism in the west and the rising nationalisms of the eastern and other dependent countries opposed this combination of fascism and imperialism. Nationalism in the East, it must be remembered, was essentially different from the new and terribly narrow nationalism of fascist countries; the former was the historical urge to freedom, the latter the last refuge of reaction.

Thus, we see the world divided up into two vast groups today—the imperialist and fascist on one side, the socialist and nationalist on the other. There is some overlapping of the two and the line between them is difficult to draw, for there is mutual conflict between the fascist and imperialist powers, and the nationalism of subject countries has sometimes a tendency to fascism. But the main division holds and if we keep it in mind, it will be easier for us to understand world conditions and our own place in them.

Where do we stand then, we who labour for a free India? Inevitably we take our stand with the progressive forces of the world which are ranged against fascism and imperialism. We have to deal with one imperialism in particular, the oldest, and the most far-reaching of the modern world, but powerful as it is, it is but one aspect of world-imperialism. And that is the final argument for Indian independence and for the severance of our connection with the British Empire. Between Indian nationalism, Indian freedom and British imperialism there can be no common ground, and if we remain within the imperialist fold, whatever our name or status, whatever outward semblance of political power we might have, we remain cribbed and confined and allied to and dominated by the reactionary forces and the great financial vested interests of the capitalist world. The exploitation of our masses will still continue and all the vital social problems that face us will remain unsolved. Even real political freedom will be out of our reach, much more so radical social changes.

With the development of this great struggle all over the world we have seen the progressive deterioration of many of the capitalist-imperialist countries and an attempt at consolidation of the reactionary forces under fascism or Naziism or so-called 'national' governments. In India, the same process has been evident to us during these past years, and the stronger the nationalist movement has grown, the more have efforts been made by our imperialist rulers to break out ranks and to gather together under their banner the reactionary elements in the country. The Round Table Conferences were such attempts and, though they helped our rulers in some measure, they served a useful purpose by showing us clearly the division between the imperialist and the anti-imperialist forces in the country. Unhappily we did not fully profit by this lesson and we still imagine that we can win over some of these imperialist groups to the side of Indian freedom and anti-imperialism, and in a vain attempt to do so, we suppress our ideals, blush for our objectives and tone down our activities.

Meanwhile the decay of British imperialism in India becomes ever more apparent. It cannot, by its very nature, solve our economic problems and rid us of our terrible poverty, which it has largely itself created.

It subsists on a normal fare of the fiercest repression and a denial of civil and even personal liberty. It surrounds us with a wide network of spies and, among the pillars of its administration, are the tribe of informers and agents provocateurs and the like. Its services try to seek comfort for their obvious deterioration and incompetence by perpetually singing songs of mutual adulation. Argument gives place to the policeman's baton and the soldier's bayonet and prison and detention camps, and even our extraordinary finances are justified by the methods of the bully. It is astonishing to find to what depths of vulgarity our rulers have descended in their ardent desire to hold on to what they have got, and it is depressing, though perhaps inevitable, that some of our countrymen, more interested in British imperialism than the British themselves, should excel at this deplorable game. So wanting in mental equilibrium are they, so obsessed by fear of the Congress and the national movement it represents, that their wishes become thoughts, their thoughts inferences, and their inferences facts, solemnly stated in official publications, and on which the majesty of the British Government rests in India, and people are kept in prison and detention camp without charge or trial. Being interested in psychology. I have watched this process of moral and intellectual decay and realised, even more than I did previously, how autocratic power corrupts and degrades and vulgarises. I have read sometimes the reports of the recent Assembly meetings and noted the great difference in tone and content between them and the Assembly of ten years ago. I have observed the forced attempts made to discredit the Congress by a reference to the Tilak Swaraj Fund with which I was connected for many years as Secretary of the Congress. But prepared as I was for much, even I was surprised at the insinuations made against our much-loved chief, Rajendra Babu, and the charges brought against the Bihar Relief Fund. A mild criticism by me of official incompetence soon after the Bihar earthquake was deeply resented probably because the truth of it was realised. Newspapers that criticised the official arrangements at a subsequent earthquake were heavily penalised or suppressed. All criticism hurts the sensitive skin of the Government and its reactions are quick and far-reaching. The more incompetent it grows the less it likes being told so. But this does not prevent it from indulging in reckless allegations about others.

This psychological aspect interests me even more than the more aggressive manifestations of British authority in India, for it throws light on much that has happened. It shows us how a clear and definite fascist mentality has developed among our rulers and how closely allied is imperialism to fascism. How this fascist mentality has functioned in the recent past and is functioning today, I shall not go into now. You know well the horror of these years and of the nightmare that we have all experienced. We shall not easily forget it and if there are some who have been cowed down by it, there are others who have steeled themselves to a greater resolve to end this infamy in India.

But of one thing I must say a few words for to me it is one of the most vital thing that I value. That is the tremendous deprivation of civil liberties in India. A government that has to rely on the Criminal Law Amendment Act and similar laws, that suppresses the press and literature, that bans hundreds of organisations, that keeps people in prison without trial and that does so many other things that are happening in India today, is a government that has ceased to have even a shadow of a justification for its existence. I can never adjust myself to these conditions, I find them intolerable. And yet I find many of my own countrymen complacent about them, some even supporting them, some who have made the practice of sitting on a fence into a fine art, being neutral when such questions are discussed. And I have wondered what there was in common between them and me and those who think like I do. We in the Congress welcome all cooperation in the struggle for Indian freedom; our doors are ever open to all who stand for that freedom and are against imperialism. But they are not open to the allies of imperialism and the supporters of repression and those who stand by the British Government in its suppression of civil liberty. We belong to opposite camps.

Recently, as you know, we have had a typical example of the way Government functions in India in the warning issued to a dear and valued comrade of ours, Subhas Chandra Bose. We who know him also know how frivolous are the charges brought against him. But even if there was substance in them we could not tolerate willingly the treatment to which he has long been subjected. He did me the honour to ask me for advice and I was puzzled and perplexed for it is no easy thing to advice another in such a matter, when such advice might mean prison. Subhas Bose has suffered enough at the cost of his health. Was I justified in adding to this mental and physical agony? I hesitated and at first suggested to him to postpone his departure. But this advice made me unhappy and I consulted other friends and then advised him differently. I suggested that he should return to his homeland as soon as he could. But it appears, that even before my advice reached him, he had started on his journey back to India.

This instance leans us to think of the larger problem, of the way the bogey of terrorism has been exploited by the Government to cruch political activity and to cripple physically and mentally the fair province of Bengal. You know that terrorism as such is practically non-existent now in Bengal or any part of India. Terrorism is always a sign of political immaturity in a people, just as so-called constitutionalism, where there is no democratic constitution, is a sign of political senility. Our national movement has long outgrown that immature stage, and even the odd individuals who have in the past indulged in terrorist acts have apparently given up that tragic and futile philosophy. The Congress, by its stress on peaceful and effective action, has drawn the youth of the country into its fold and all traces of terroristic activity would long have vanished but for the policy of the Government which feeds the roots out of which a helpless violence grows. But terrorism or no terrorism, a government which adopts the methods which have long prevailed in Midnapore and elsewhere in Bengal stands self-condemned. Similar methods have also long prevailed in the Frontier Province, although there is no hint of terroristic activity there, and the fine man and true, beloved of millions, Abdul Ghaffar Khan, still lies in prison. Excuses differ, but the real reason is the ever-growing fascist mentality of our rulers.

That is one side of the picture. What of us? I have found a spirit of disunion spreading over the land, a strange malaise, and petty conflicts amongst old comrades growing ever bigger and interfering in all activity. We have forgotten for the moment the larger ideals we stood for and we quarrel over petty issues. We have largely lost touch with the masses and, deprived of the life giving energy that flows from them, we dry up and weaken and our organisation shrinks and loses the power it had. First things must always come first and because we have forgotten this and argue and dispute over secondary matters, we are in danger of losing our bearings.

Every great struggle has its ups and downs and temporary failures. When such a setback occurs there is a reaction when the funds of national energy is exhausted and has to be re-charged. That happens again and yet that is not an adequate explanation of all that has taken place. Our direct action struggles in the past were based on the masses, and especially the peasantry, but the backbone and leadership were always supplied by the middle classes, and this, under the circumstances, was inevitable. The middle classes are vague group or groups; at the top, a handful of them are closely allied to British imperialism; at the bottom are the dispossessed and other groups who have been progressively crushed by economic circumstances and out of whose ranks come the advanced political workers and revolutionaries; in between are the centre groups, which tend often to side with the advanced elements, but which also have alliances with the upper groups and live in the hope of joining their superior ranks. A middle class leadership is thus often a distracted leadership, looking in two directions at the same time. In times of crisis and struggle, when unity of aim and activity is essential, this two-faced leadership is bound to injure the cause and to hold back when a forward move is called for. Being too much tied up with property and the goods of this world, it is fearful of losing them, and it is easier to bring pressure on it and to exhaust its stamina. And yet, paradoxically, it is only from the middle class intellectuals that revolutionary leadership comes, and we in India know that our bravest leaders and our stoutest comrades have come from the ranks of the middle classes. But by the very nature of our struggle, these front-rank leaders are taken away and the others who take their place tire and are influenced more by the static element of their classes. That has been very evident during our recent struggle when our propertied classes were hit hard by the Government's drastic policy of seizure and confiscation of monies and properties, and were thus induced to bring pressure for the suspension of the struggle.

How is this problem to be solved then? Inevitably, we must have middle class leadership but this must look more and more towards the masses and draw strength and inspiration from them. The Congress must be not only for the masses, as it claims to be, but of the masses; only then will it really be for the masses. I have a feeling that our relative weakness today is due to a certain decay of our middle class elements and our divorce from the people at large. Our policies and ideas are governed far more by this middle class outlook than by a consideration of the needs of the great majority of the population. Even the problems that trouble us are essentially middle class problems, like the communal problem, which have no significance for the masses.

This is partly due, I think, to a certain historical growth during that last fifteen years to which we have failed to adapt ourselves, to a growing urgency of economic problems affecting the masses, and to a rising mass consciousness which does not find sufficient outlet through the Congress. This was not so in 1920 and later when there was an organic link between Congress and the masses, and their needs and desires, vague as they were, found expression in the Congress. But as those needs and desires have taken more definite shape, they have not been so welcome to other elements in the Congress and the organic connection has gone. That, though regrettable, is really a sign of growth and, instead of lamenting it, we must find a new link and a new connection on a fresh basis which allows for growth of mass consciousness within the Congress. The middle class claim to represent the masses had some justification in 1920; it has much less today, though the lower middle classes have still a great deal in common with the masses.

Partly also our divorce from the people at large is due to a certain narrowness of our Congress constitution. The radical changes made in it fifteen years ago brought it in line with existing conditions then and it drew in large numbers and became an effective instrument of national activity. Though the control and background were essentially middle-class and city, it reached the remotest village and brought with it political and economic consciousness to the masses and there was widespread discussion of national issues in city and village alike. One could feel the new life pulsating through the vast land of ours and, as we were in harmony with it, we drew strength from it. The intense repression by the Government during later years broke many of our physical and outward bonds with our countryside. But something more than that happened. The vague appeal of earlier days no longer sufficed, and on the new economic issues that were forcing themselves on us, we hesitated to give a definite opinion. Worse even than the physical divorce, there was a mental divorce between the middle class elements and the mass elements. Our constitution no longer fitted in with changing conditions; it lost its roots in the soil and became a matter of small committees functioning in the air. It still had the mighty prestige of the Congress name behind it and this carried it a long way, but it had lost the living democratic touch. It became a prey to authoritarianism and a battleground for rival cliques fighting for control, and, in doing so, stooping to the lowest and most objectionable of tactics. Idealism disappeared and in its place there came opportunism and corruption. The constitutional structure of the Congress was unequal to facing the new situation; it could be shaken up anywhere almost by a handful unscrupulous individuals. Only a broad democratic basis could have saved it and this was lacking.

Last year an attempt was made to revise the constitution in order to get rid of some of these evils. How far that attempt has succeeded or not I am not competent to judge. Perhaps it has made the organisation more efficient but efficiency means little if it has no strength behind it, and strength, for us, can only come from the masses. The present constitution stresses still further the authoritarian side of the organisation, and in spite of stressing rural representation, does not provide effective links with the masses.

The real problem for us is, how in our struggle for independence we can join together all the anti-imperialist forces in the country, how we can make a broad front of our mass elements with the great majority of the middle classes which stands for independence. There has been some talk of a joint front but, so far as I can gather, this refers to some alliance among the upper classes, probably at the expense of the masses. That surely can never be the idea of the Congress and, if it favours it, it betrays the interests it has claimed to represent, and loses the very reason for its existence. The essence of a joint popular front must be uncompromising opposition to imperialism and the strength of it must inevitably come from the active participation of the peasantry and workers.

Perhaps you have wondered at the way I have dealt at some length with the background of international and national affairs and not touched so far the immediate problems that fill your minds. You may have grown impatient. But I am convinced that the only right way of looking at our own problems is to see them in their proper place in a world-setting. I am convinced that there is intimate connection between world events, and our national problem is but a part of the world problem of capitalist-imperialism. To look at each event apart from the others and without understanding the connection between them must lead us to the formation of erratic and erroneous views. Look at the vast panorama of world change today, where mighty forces are at grips with each other and dreadful war darkens the horizon. Subject peoples struggling for freedom and imperialism crushing them down; exploited classes facing their exploiters and seeking freedom and equality. Italian imperialism bombing and killing the brave Ethiopians; Japanese imperialism continuing its aggression in North China and Mongolia; British imperialism piously objecting to other countries misbehaving, yet carrying on in much the same way in India and the Frontier; and behind it all a decaying economic order which intensifies all these conflicts. Can we not see an organic connection in all these various phenomena? Let us try to develop the historic sense so that we can view current events in proper perspective and understand their real significance. Only then we can appreciate the march of history and keep step with it.

I realise that in this address I am going a little beyond the usual beat of the Congress president. But I do not want you to have me under any false pretences and we must have perfect frankness with each other. Most of you must know my views on social and economic matters for I have often given expression to them. Yet you chose me as president. I do not take that choice to mean an endorsement by you all, or by a majority, of those views, but I take it that this does mean that those views are spreading in India and that most of you will be indulgent in considering them at least.

I am convinced that the only key to the solution of the world's problems and of India's problems lies in socialism, and when I use this word I do so not in a vague humanitarian way but in the scientific, economic sense. Socialism is, however, something even more than an economic doctrine, it is a philosophy of life and as such also it appeals to me. I see no way of ending the poverty, the vast unemployment, the degradation and the subjection of the Indian people except through socialism. That involves vast and revolutionary changes in our political and social structure, the ending of vested interests in land and industry, as well as the feudal and autocratic Indian states system. That means the ending of private property, except in a restricted sense, and the replacement of the present profit system by a higher ideal of cooperative service It means ultimately a change in our instincts and habits and desires. In short, it means a new civilisation, radically different from the capitalist order. Some glimpse we can have of this new civilisation in the territories of the USSR. Much has happened there which has pained me greatly and with which I disagree, but I look upon that great and fascinating unfolding of a new order and a new civilisation as the most promising feature of our dismal age. If the future is full of hope, it is largely because of Soviet Russia and what it has done, and I am convinced that, if some world catastrophe does not intervene, this new civilisation will spread to other lands and put an end to the wars and conflicts which capitalism feeds.

I do not know how or when this new order will come to India. I imagine that every country will fashion it after its own way and fit it in with its national genius. But the essential basis of that order must remain and be a link in the world order that will emerge out of the present chaos.

Socialism is thus for me not merely an economic doctrine which I favour; it is a vital creed which I hold with all my head and heart.

I work for Indian independence because the nationalist in me cannot tolerate alien domination; I work for it even more because for me it is the inevitable step to social and economic change. I should like the Congress to become a socialist organisation and to join hands with the other forces in the world who are working for the new civilisation. But I realise that the majority in the Congress, as it is constituted today, may not be prepared to go thus far. We are a nationalist organisation and we think and work on the nationalist plane. It is evident enough now that this is too narrow even for the limited objective of political independence, and so we talk of the masses and their economic needs. But still most of us hesitate, because of our nationalist backgrounds, to take a step which might frighten away some vested interests. Most of those interests are already ranged against us and we can expect little from them except opposition even in the political struggle.

Much as I wish for the advancement of socialism in this country, I have no desire to force the issue in the Congress and thereby create difficulties in the way of our struggle for independence. I shall cooperate gladly and with all the strength in me with all those who work for independence even though they do not agree with the socialist solution. But I shall do so stating my position frankly and hoping in course of time to convert the Congress and the country to it, for only thus can I see it achieving independence. It should surely be possible for all of us who believe in independence to join our ranks together even though we might differ on the social issue. The Congress has been in the past a broad front representing various opinions joined together by that common bond. It must continue as such even though the difference of those opinions becomes more marked.

How does socialism fit in with the present ideology of the Congress? I do not think it does. I believe in the rapid industrialisation of the country and only thus I think will the standards of the people rise substantially and poverty be combated. Yet I have cooperated wholeheartedly in the past with the *Khadi* programme and I hope to do so in the future because I believe that *Khadi* and village industries have a definite place in our present economy. They have a social, a political and an economic value which is difficult to measure but which is apparent enough to those who have studied their effects. But I look upon them more as temporary expedients of a transition stage rather than as solutions of our vital problems. That stage might be a long one, and in a country like India, village industries might well play an important, though subsidiary, role even after the development of industrialism. But though I cooperate in the village industries programme my ideological approach to it differs considerably from that of many others in the Congress who are opposed to industrialisation and socialism.

The problem of untouchability and the Harijans again can be approached in different ways. For a socialist it presents no difficulty for under socialism there can be no such differentiation or victimisation. Economically speaking, the Harijans have constituted the landless proletariat and an economic solution removes the social barriers that custom and tradition have raised.

I come now to a question which is probably occupying your minds—the new Act passed by the British Parliament and our policy in regard to it. This Act has come into being since the last Congress met, but even at that time we had a foretaste of it in the shape of the White Paper, and I know of no abler analysis of those provisions than that contained in the presidential address of my predecessor in this high office. The Congress rejected that proposed constitution and resolved to have nothing to do with it. The new Act, as is well known, is an even more retrograde measure and has been condemned by even the most moderate and cautious of our politicians. If we rejected the White Paper, what then are we to do with this new charter of slavery to strengthen the bonds of imperialist domination and to intensify the exploitation of our masses? And even if we forget its content for a while, can we forget the insult and injury that have accompanied it, the contemptuous defiance of our wishes, the suppression of civil liberties and the widespread repression that has been our normal lot? If they had offered to us the crown of heaven with this accompaniment and with dishonour, would we not have spurned it as inconsistent with our national honour and self-respect? What then of this?

A charter of slavery is no law for the slave, and though we may perforce submit for a while to it and to the humiliation of ordinances and the like, inherent in that enforced submission is the right and the desire to rebel against it and to end it.

Our lawyers have examined this new constitution and have condemned it. But constitutions are something much more than legal documents. 'The real constitution', said Ferdin and Lassalle, consists of 'the actual relationships of power', and the working of this power we see even today, after the Act has been passed. That is the constitution we have to face, not the fine phrases which are sometimes presented to us, and we can only deal with it with the strength and power generated by the people of the country.

To this Act our attitude can only be one of uncompromising hostility and a constant endeavour to end it. How can we do this?

Since my return from Europe I have had the advantage of full and frank discussion with my colleagues of the Working Committee. All of us have agreed that the Act has to be rejected and combated but all of us have not been able to agree to the manner of doing so. We have pulled together in the past and I earnestly hope that we shall do so in the future, but in order to do so effectively we must recognise that there are marked differences in our outlooks. I do not yet know, as I write what the final recommendation of the Working Committee will be on this issue. I can only, therefore, venture to put before you my own personal views on the subject, not knowing how far they represent the views of Congressmen. I should like to make it clear; however, in fairness to my old colleagues of the Working Committee, that the majority of them do not agree with all the views I am going to express. But whether we agree or disagree, or whether we agree to differ, there is a strong desire on our part to continue to cooperate together, laying stress on our many points of agreement rather than on the differences. That is the right course for us and, as a democratic organisation, that is the only course open to us.

I think that, under the circumstances, we have no choice but to contest the election to the new provincial legislatures, in the event of their taking place. We should seek election on the basis of a detailed political and economic programme, with our demand for a Constituent Assembly in the fore-front. I am convinced that the only solution of our political and communal problems will come through such an Assembly, provided it is elected on an adult franchise and a mass basis. That Assembly will not come into existence till at least a semi-revolutionary situation has been created in this country and the actual relationships of power, apart from paper constitutions, are such that the people of India can make their will felt. When that will happen I cannot say, but the world is too much in the grip of dynamic forces today to admit of static conditions in India or elsewhere for long. We may thus have to face this issue sooner than we might expect. But, obviously, a Constituent Assembly will not come through the new Act or the new legislatures. Yet we must press this demand and keep it before our country and the world, so that when the time comes we may be ripe for it.

A Constituent Assembly is the only proper and democratic method for the framing of our constitution, and for its delegates then to negotiate a treaty with the representatives of the British Government. But we cannot go to it with blank minds in the hope that something good will emerge out of it. Such an Assembly, in order to be fruitful, must have previous thought behind it and a definite scheme put forward by an organised group. The actual details, as to how the Assembly is to be convened, must depend on the circumstances then existing and need not trouble us now. But it will be our function as the Congress to know exactly what we are after, to place this clearly and definitely before the Assembly, and to press for its acceptance.

One of the principal reasons for our seeking election will be to carry the message of the Congress to the millions of voters and to the scores of millions, of the disfranchised, to acquaint them with our future programme and policy, to make the masses realise that we not only stand for them but that we are of them and seek to cooperate with them in removing their social and economic burdens. Our appeal and message will not be limited to the voters, for we must remember that hundreds of millions are disfranchised and they need our help most for they are at the bottom of the social ladder and suffer most from exploitation. We have seen in the past wide-spread official interference in the elections; we shall have to face that, as well as the serried and monied ranks of the reactionaries. But the real danger will come from our toning down our programme and policy in order to win over the hesitating and compromising groups and individuals. If we compromise on principles, we shall fall between two stools and deserve our fall. The only right way and the only safe way is to stand four-square on our own programme and to compromise with no one who has opposed the national struggle for freedom in the past, or who is in any way giving support to British imperialism.

When we have survived the election, what then are we to do? Office or no office? A secondary matter perhaps, and yet behind that issue lie deep questions of principle and vital differences of outlook, and a decision on that, either way, has far-reaching consequences. Behind it lies, somewhat hidden, the question of independence itself and whether we seek revolutionary changes in India or are working for petty reforms under the aegis of British imperialism. We go back again in thought to the clash of ideas which preceded the changes in the Congress in 1920. We made a choice then deliberately and with determination and discarded the old sterile creed of reformism. Are we to go back again to that blind and suffocating lane, after all these years of brave endeavour, and to wipe out the memory of what we have done and achieved and suffered? That is the issue and let none of us forget it when we have to give our decision. In this India, crying aloud for radical and fundamental change, in this world pregnant with revolutionary and dynamic possibility, are we to forget our mission and our historic, destiny, and slide back to static futility? And if some of us feel tired and hunger for rest and quiet, do we imagine that India's masses will follow our lead, when elemental forces and economic necessity are driving them to their inevitable goal? If we enter the backwaters, others will take our place on the bosom of the flowing stream and will dare to take the rapids and ride the torrent.

How has this question arisen? If we express our hostility to the Act and reject the entire scheme; does it not follow logically that we should have nothing to do with the working of it and should prevent its functioning in so far as we can? To accept office and ministry, under the conditions of Act, is to negative our rejection of it and to stand self-condemned. National honour and self-respect cannot accept this position, for it would inevitably mean our cooperation in some measure with the repressive apparatus of imperialism, and we would become partners in this repression and in the exploitation of our people. Of course, we would try to champion the rights of the people and would protest against repression, but as ministers under the Act, we could do very little to give relief, and we would have to share responsibility for the administration with the apparatus of imperialism, for the deficit budgets, for the suppression of labour and the peasantry. It is always dangerous to assume responsibility without power, even in democratic countries; it will be far worse with this undemocratic constitution, hedged in with safeguards and reserved powers and mortgaged funds, where we have to follow the rules and regulations of our opponents' making. Imperialism sometimes talks of cooperation but the kind of cooperation it wants is usually known as surrender, and the ministers who accept office will have to do so at the price of surrender of much that they might have stood for in public. That is a humiliating position which self-respect itself should prevent one from accepting. For our great national organisation to be party to it is to give up the very basis and background of our existence.

Self-respect apart, common sense tells us that we can lose much and gain little by acceptance of office in terms of the Act. We cannot get much out of it, or else our criticism of the Act itself is wrong, and we know that it is not so. The big things for which we stand will fade into the background and petty issues will absorb our attention, and we shall lose ourselves in compromises and communal tangles, and disillusion with us will spread over the land. If we have a majority, and only then can the question of acceptance of office arise, we shall be in a position to dominate the situation and to prevent reactionaries and imperialists from profiting by it. Office will not add to our real strength, it will only weaken us by making us responsible for many thinkgs that we utterly dislike.

Again, if we are in a minority, the question of office does not arise. It may be, however, that we are on the verge of a majority and with the cooperation of other individuals and groups we can obtain office. There is nothing inherently wrong in our acting together with others on specific issues of civil liberty or economic or other demands, provided we do not compromise on any principle. But I can imagine few things more dangerous and more likely to injure us than the acceptance of office on the sufferance of others. That would be an intolerable position.

It is said that our chances at the elections would increase if we announced that we were prepared to accept offices and ministries. Perhaps that might be so for all manner of other people, eager for the spoils and patronage that office gives, would then hurry to join us. Does any Congressman imagine that this would be a desirable development or that we would gain strength thereby? Again it is said more voters would vote for us if they knew that we were going to form ministries. That might happen if we deluded them with false promises of what we might do for them within the Act, but a quick nemesis would follow our failure to give effect to those promises, and failure would be inevitable if the promises were worthwhile.

There is only one straight course open to us, to go to the people with our programme and make it clear to them that we cannot give effect to the major items in it under present conditions, and therefore, while we use the platform of the legislatures to press that programme, we seek to end these imperialist bodies by creating deadlocks in them whenever we are in a position to do so. Those deadlocks should preferably take place on those programmes so that the masses might learn how ineffective for their purpose are these legislatures.

One fact is sometimes forgotten—the provision for second chambers in many of the provinces. These chambers will be reactionary and will be exploited by the Governor to check any forward tendencies in the lower house. They will make the position of a minister, who seeks advance, even more difficult and unenviable.

Some people have suggested, though their voices are hushed now, that provincial autonomy might be given on this office issue and each Provincial Congress Committee should be empowered to decide it for its own province. An astonishing and fatal suggestion playing into the hands of our imperialist rulers. We who have laboured for Indian unity can never be parties to any proposal which tends to lessen that unity. That way lies disaster and a disruption of the forces working for freedom. If we agree to this, why then should we also not agree to the communal issue being decided provincially, or many other issues, where individual provinces might think differently? First issues will sink into the background, independence itself will fade away, and the narrowest provincialism raise its ugly head. Our policy must be uniform for the whole of India, and it must place first things first, and independence is the first thing of all.

So that I am convinced that for the Congress to favour the acceptance of office, or even to hesitate and waver about it, would be a vital error. It will be a pit from which it would be difficult for us to come out. Practical statesmanship is against it, as well as the traditions of the Congress and the mentality we have sought to develop in the people. Psychologically, any such lead might have disastrous consequences. If we stand for revolutionary changes, as we do, we have to cultivate a revolutionary mentality among our people, and anything that goes against it is harmful to our cause.

This psychological aspect is important. For we must never forget, and never delude our masses into imagining, that we can get any real power or real freedom through working these legislatures. We may use them certainly to advance our cause to some extent, but the burden of the struggle for freedom must fall on the masses, and primarily, therefore, our effective work must lie outside these legislatures. Strength will come from the masses and from our work among them and our organisation of them.

Of secondary importance though the work in the legislatures is, we may not treat it casually and allow it to become a hindrance to our other work. Therefore, it is necessary for the Congress, through its executive, to have direct control over the elections and the programme placed before the country, as well as the activity in the legislatures. Such control will inevitably be exercised through committees and boards appointed for the purpose, but the continued existence of semi-autonomous parliamentary boards seems to be undesirable. Provision should also be made for a periodical review of all such activities so that Congressmen in general and the country should keep in touch with them and should influence them.

We have considered the provincial elections which, it is said, may take place early next year. The time is far off yet and it is by no means impossible that these elections may not take place for a much longer time, or may not take place at all, and the new Act may take its rightful place in oblivion. Much may happen in the course of the next year, and war is ever on the horizon, to upset the schemes and time-tables of our rulers. But we cannot speculate on this and we have to make provision for contingencies. That decision might even have been delayed, the dangerous and compromising tendencies seek to influence Congress policy, and the Congress cannot remain silent when the issue is raised and its whole future is in the balance.

The provincial legislatures may come, but few persons, I imagine, are confident about the coming of the federal part of this unholy structure. So far as we are concerned we shall fight against it to our utmost strength, and the primary object of our creating deadlocks in the provinces and making the new Act difficult of functioning, is to kill the Federation. With the Federation dead, the provincial end of the Act will also go and leave the slate clean for the people of India to write on. That writing, whatever it be, can never admit the right of the Indian states to continue as feudal and autocratic monarchies. They have long survived their day, propped up by an alien Power, and have become the strongest anomalies in a changing world. The future has no place for autocracy or feudalism; a free India cannot tolerate the subjection of many of her children and their deprivation of human rights, nor can it ever agree to a dissection of its body and a cutting up of its limbs. If we stand for any human, political, social or economic rights for ourselves, we stand for those identical rights for the people of the states.

I have referred to the terrible suppression of civil liberties by the British Government in India. But in the states matters are even worse, and though we know that the real power behind those states is that British imperialism, this tragic suppression of our brothers by their own countrymen is of painful significance. Indian Rulers and their ministers have spoken and acted increasingly in the approved fascist manner, and their record during the past few years especially has been one of aggressive opposition to our national demands. States which are considered advanced ban the Congress organisation and offer insult to our national flag, and decree new laws to suppress the press. What shall we say of the more backward and primitive states?

There is one more matter concerning the Constitution Act which has given rise to much controversy. This is the communal decision. Many people have condemned it strongly and, I think, rightly; few have a good word for it. My own view-point is, however, somewhat different from that of others. I am not concerned so much with what it gives to this group or that but more so with the basic idea behind it. It seeks to divide India into numerous separate compartments, chiefly on a religious basis, and thus makes the development of democracy and economic policy very difficult. Indeed, the communal decision and democracy can never go together. We have to admit that, under present circumstances, and so long as our politics are dominated by middle class elements, we cannot do away with communalism altogether. But to make a necessary exception in favour of our Muslim or Sikh friends is one thing, to spread this evil principle to numerous other groups and thus to divide up the electoral machinery and the legislature into many compartments, is a far more dangerous proposition. If we wish to function democratically the proposed communal arrangement will have to go, and I have no doubt that it will go. But it will not go by the methods adopted by the aggressive opponents of the decision. These methods result inevitably in perpetuating the decision for they help in continuing a situation which prevents any reconsideration.

I have not been enamoured of the past Congress policy in regard to the communal question and its attempts to make pacts and compromises. Yet essentially I think it was based on a sound instinct. First of all, the Congress always put independence first and other questions, including the communal one, second, and refused to allow any of those other questions to take pride of place. Secondly, it argued that the communal problem had arisen from a certain set of circumstances which enabled the third party to exploit the other two. In order to solve it, one had either to get rid of the third party (and that meant independence), or get rid of that set of circumstances, which meant a friendly approach by the parties concerned and an attempt to soften the prejudice and fear that filled them. Thirdly, that the majority community must show generosity in the matter to allay the fear and suspicion that minorities, even though unreasonably, might have.

That analysis is I think perfectly sound. I would add that, in my opinion, a real solution of the problem will only come when economic issues, affecting all religious groups and cutting across communal boundaries, arise. Apart from the upper middle classes, who live in hopes of office and patronage, the masses and the lower middle classes have to face identical political and economic problems. It is odd and significant that all the communal demands of any group, of which so much is heard, have nothing whatever to do with these problems of the masses and the lower middle classes.

It is also significant that the principal communal leaders, Hindu or Moslem or others, are political reactionaries, quite apart from the communal question. It is sad to think how they have sided with British imperialism in vital matters, how they have given their approval to the suppression of civil liberty, how during these years of agony they have sought to gain narrow profit for their group at the expense of the larger cause of freedom. With them there can be no cooperation, for that would mean cooperation with reaction. But I am sure that with the larger masses and the middle classes, who may have temporarily been led away by the specious claims of their communal leaders, there must be the fullest cooperation, and out of that cooperation will come a fairer solution of this problem.

I am afraid I cannot get excited over this communal issue, important as it is temporary. It is after all a side issue and it can have no real importance in the larger scheme of things. Those who think of it as the major issue, think in terms of British imperialism continuing permanently in this country. Without that basis of thought, they would not attach so much importance to one of its inevitable off shoots. I ave no such fear and so my vision of a future India contains neither imperialism nor communalism.

Yet the present difficulty remains and has to be faced. Especially our sympathy must go to the people of Bengal who have suffered most from these communal decisions, as well as from the heavy hand of the Government. Whenever opportunity offers to improve their situation in a friendly way, we must seize it. But always the background of our action must be the national struggle for independence and the social freedom of the masses.

I have referred previously to the growing divorce between our organisation and the masses. Individually, many of us still have influence with the masses and our word carries weight with them, and who can measure the love and reverence of India's millions for our leader, Gandhiji? And yet organisationally we have lost that intimate touch that we had. The social reform activities of the *khadi* and village industries and Harijan organisations keep large numbers of our comrades in touch with the masses and those contacts bear fruit. But they are essentially non-political and so, politically, we have largely lost touch.

There are many reasons for this and some are beyond our control. Our present Congress constitution is, I feel, not helpful in developing these contacts or in encouraging enough the democratic spirit in its primary committees. These committees are practically rolls of voters who meet only to elect delegates or representatives, and take no part in discussion or the formation of policy.

It is interesting to read in that monumental and impressive record, the Web's new book on Russia, how the whole Soviet structure is based on a wide and living democratic foundation. Russia is not supposed to be a democratic country after the Western pattern, and yet we find the essentials of democracy present in far greater degree amongst the masses there than anywhere else. The six hundred thousand towns and villages there have a vast democratic organisation, each with its own soviet, constantly discussing, debating, criticising, helping in the formulation of policy, electing representatives to higher committees. This organisation of citizens covers the entire population over 18 years of age. There is yet another vast organisation of the people as producers, and a third, equally vast as consumers. And thus scores of millions of men and women are constantly taking part in the discussion of public affairs and actually in the administration of the country. There has been no such practical application of the democratic process in history.

All this is of course utterly beyond us, for it requires a change in the political and economic structure and much else before we can experiment that way. But we can profit by that example still and try in our own limited way to develop democracy in the lowest rungs of the Congress ladder and make the primary committee a living organisation.

An additional method for us to increase our contacts with the masses is to organise them as producers and then affiliate such organisations to the Congress or have full cooperation between the two. Such organisations of producers as exist today, such as trade unions and peasant unions, as well as other anti-imperialist organisation could also be brought within this sphere of mutual cooperation for the good of the masses and for the struggle for national freedom. Thus, Congress could have an individual as well as a corporate membership, and retaining its individual character, could influence, and be influenced by, other mass elements.

These are big changes that I have hinted at, and I am by no means sure how they can be brought about, or whether it is possible to go far in this direction in the near future. Still we must move to some extent at least if we are to have our roots in the soil of India and draw life and strength from its millions. The subject is fascinating but complicated and can only be tackled by an expert committee which I trust will be appointed on behalf of the Congress. The report of that committee must be freely discussed so as to get the widest backing for it.

All this will take us to the next Congress. Meanwhile perhaps some urgent changes are needed in our constitution to remove anomalies and avoid difficulties. Owing to my absence I have had little experience of the working of the new constitution and cannot make any concrete suggestions. The reduction in the number of delegates and A.I.C.C. members would be, to some extent, desirable if there was a background of widespread activity in the primary and secondary committee. Without it, it makes us even less responsive to mass opinion, and, therefore, an increase seems desirable. But the real solution is to increase the interest and day-to-day activity of the lower committees.

I have been told that the manual labour franchise has not been a success and has led to a great deal of evasion. If that is so a change is desirable for a constitution must be such as can be worked easily and without subterfuge.

The Congress is an all-inclusive body and represents many interests, but, essentially it is a political organisation with various subsidiary and allied organisations, like the Spinners' Association and the Village Industries Association. These allied organisations work in the economic field but they do not seek directly to remove the burdens of the peasantry under the present system of land tenure. Nor can the Congress, situated as it is, wholly function as a peasant organisation, although in many provinces it has espoused the cause of the peasantry and brought them much relief. It seems to me necessary that the Congress should encourage the formation of peasant's unions as well as workers' unions and cooperate with such as already exist, so that the day-to-day struggle of the masses might be carried on the basis of their economic demands and other grievances. This identification of the Congress with the economic struggle of the masses will bring us nearer to them and nearer to freedom than anything else. I would welcome also the organisation of other special interests, like those of the women, in the general framework of our national struggle for freedom. The Congress would be in a position to coordinate all these vital activities and thus to base itself on the widest possible mass foundation.

There has been some talk of a militant programme and militant action. I do not know what exactly is meant, but if direct action on a national scale or civil disobedience are meant, then I would say that I see no near prospect of them. Let us not indulge in tall talk before we are ready for big action. Our business today is to put our house in order, to sweep away the defeatist mentality of some people, and to build up our organisation with its mass affiliations as well as to work amongst the masses. The time may come, and that sooner perhaps than we expect, when we might be put to the test. Let us get ready for that test. Civil disobedience and the like cannot be switched on and off when we feel like doing so. It depends on many things, some of which are beyond our control, but in these days of revolutionary change and constantly recurring crises in the world, events often move faster than we do. We shall not lack for opportunities.

The major problem of India today is that of the—rural poverty and unemployment and a thoroughly cut-of-date land system. A curious combination of circumstances has held back India during the past few generations and the political and economic garments it wears no longer fit it and are torn and tattered. In some ways our agrarian conditions are not unlike those of France a hundred and fifty years ago, prior to the great revolution. They cannot continue so far long. At the same time we have become parts of international capitalism and we suffer the pains and crises which afflict this decaying system. As a result of these elemental urges and conflicts of world forces what will emerge in India none can say. But we can say with confidence that the present order has reached the evening of its day, and it is up to us to try to mould the future as we would like it to be.

The world is filled with rumours and alarms of war. In Abyssinia bloody and cruel war has already gone on for many months and we have watched anew how hungry and predatory imperialism behaves in its mad search for colonial domains. We have watched also with admiration the brave fight of the Ethopians for their freedom against heavy odds. You will permit me, I feel sure, to greet them on your behalf and express our deep sympathy for them. Their struggle is something more than a local struggle. It is one of the first effective checks by an African people on an advancing imperialism and already it has had far-reaching consequences.

In the Far East also war hovers on the horizon and we see an eastern imperialism advancing methodically and pitilessly over ancient China and dreaming of world empire. Imperialism shows its claws wherever it may be, in the West or in the East.

In Europe, an aggressive fascism or Nazism steps continuously on the brink of war and vast armed camps arise in preparation för what seems to be the inevitable end of all this. Nation join hand to fight other nations, and progressive forces in each country ally themselves to fight the fascist menace.

Where do we come in this awful game? What part shall we play in this approaching tragedy? It is difficult to say. But we must not permit ourselves to be passive tools exploited for imperialist ends. It must be our right to say whether we join a war or not, and without that consent there should be no-cooperation from us. When the time comes we may have little say in the matter, and so it becomes necessary for the Congress to declare clearly now its opposition to India's participation in any imperialist war, and every war that will be waged by imperialist powers will be an imperialist war, whatever the excuses put forward might be. Therefore, we must keep out of it and not allow Indian lives and Indian money to be sacrificed.

To the progressive forces of the world, to those who stand for human freedom and the breaking of political and social bonds, we offer our full cooperation in their struggle against imperialism and fascist reaction, for we realise that our struggle is a common one. Our grievance is not against any people or any country as such, and we know that even in imperialist England, which throttles us, there are many who do not love imperialism and who stand for freedom.

During this period of difficulty and stress and strain, inevitably our minds and hearts turn to our great leader who has guided us and inspired us by his dynamic personality these many years. Physical ill-health prevents him now from taking his full share in public activities. Our good wishes go out to him for his rapid and complete recovery, and with those wishes is the selfish desire to have him back again amongst us. We have differed from him in the past and we shall differ from in the future about many things, and it is right that each one of us should act up to his convictions. But the bonds that hold us together are stronger and more vital than our differences, and the pledges we took together still ring in our ears. How many of us have that passionate desire for Indian independence and the raising of our poverty-stricken masses which consumes him? Many things he taught us long years ago it seems now fearlessness and discipline and the will to sacrifice ourselves for the longest cause. That lesson may have grown dim but we have not forgotten it, nor can we ever forget him who has made us what we are and raised India again from the depths. The pledge of independence that we took together still remains to be redeemed, and we await again for him to guide us with wise counsel.

But no leader, however great he be, can shoulder the burden single-handed; we must all share it to the best of our ability and not seek helplessly to rely on others to perform miracles. Leaders come and go; many of our best-loved captains and comrades have left us all too soon, but India goes on and so does India's struggle for freedom. It may be that many of us must suffer still and die so that India may live and be free. The promised land may yet be far from us and we may have to march wearily through the deserts, but who will take away from us that deathless hope which has survived the scaffold and immeasurable suffering and sorrow; who will dare to crush the spirit of India which has found re-birth again and again after so many crucifications?

6

ON RELIGION AND POLITICS

Nehru was one of the most fascinating political leaders of the period from 1922 to 1964. His position in the nationalist movement was next only to that of Gandhiji, in India. When India became independent in 1947, Nehru became the Prime Minister, a position which he occupied until his death in 1964. Very few leaders of the national liberation movements of the post-1945 era have had such a long tenure in office. He was not famous for originating a new political party or for expounding a new political philosophy, but there were few political events and ideas of his times on which he did not express himself. His reaction to racialism, imperialism, nationalism, capitalism, socialism and fascism were coherently revealed in many of his works and he influenced a large number of people in India and also those in other countries. He became the symbol of Asian resurgence and he associated himself with the national liberation movements and antiracialism in Africa.

Nehru had a great share in the shaping of the nationalist movement. He was greatly influenced by Gandhiji. His early education in England also made him to accept some of the ideas of European liberalism of the early nineteenth century and the early twentieth century. He said, "I am very far from being a communist. My roots are still partly in the nineteenth century, and I have been too much influenced by the humanist liberal tradition to get out of it completely. The bourgeois background shows and follows me around and is naturally an irritation to many communists. I dislike dogmatism and the treatment of Karl Marx's writings or any other book as a revealed scripture which cannot be challenged and the regimentation and heavy hunts which seems to be a feature of modern communism".[1] The liberalism of West Europeans, and particularly that of the Englishmen influenced him. He noted that unlike the British liberals, the Indian liberals were without any economic foundation. He did not have any resentment against these liberals. He associated them in a big way with the framing of the Indian Constitution.

Nehru's commitment to non-violence was not total. He criticised Gandhiji for his use of fasts as a political weapon. He said, "Again I watched the emotional upheaval of the country during the fast, and I wondered more and more if this was the right method in politics. It seemed to be sheer revivalism, and clear thinking had not a ghost of chance against it. All India, or most of it, started reverently at the Mahatma and expected him to perform miracle after miracle and put an end to untouchability and get *Swaraj* and so on and did precious little itself".[2] He never rebelled against Gandhiji and also never condemned the political record of Gandhiji. He understood Gandhiji. He was never a mechanical and blind follower of Gandhiji. He maintained that coercion might be preferred to conversion on some occasions. In the last phase of his life, he was moving towards the Gandhian views. He preferred for the extensive use of science and technology for the economic reconstruction of India.

India has emerged as a middle power in the international field. This was possible because of the foundations of independent India laid down by Nehru. When India was fighting for freedom, he was emphasising the theme that freedom was indivisible. And he was always connected with the struggle of Indians for freedom and equality with similar struggles elsewhere. In 1946 he said, "We propose as far as possible, to keep away from the power politics of the groups, aligned against one another, which have led in the past to two World Wars and which may again lead to disaster on an even vaster scale".[3] Again in 1948, he said, "Now I am not talking in terms of this bloc or that bloc; I am talking independently of the blocs as they have appeared on the world stage. We have either to pursue our policy generally within limitations because we cannot pursue it whole-heartedly, nevertheless openly—or give it up. I do not think that anything would be more injurious to us from any point of view, but equally so from the point of view of opportunism and national interest in the narrowest sense of the word than to give up the policies we have pursued, namely, those of standing up to certain ideals in regard to . . . oppressed nations ourselves with this great power or that and becoming its camp follower in the hope that some crumb might fall from the table".[4]

One important contribution made by Nehru to India was his popularisation of the use of science and technology in the economic field. He organised the building of large dams and the extensive use of fertilisers and new seeds. He always opposed some Indian communists who advocated bloody revolutions through the dictatorship of the proletariat. He comprehended the relevance of mixed economy for increasing production in an underdeveloped country like India. His secularism went beyond Gandhi's anti-communalism. He did not stop with saying that all religions were true, but maintained that religion had no part to play in public life in general and in politics in particular. He thought that India must imbibe the scientific culture of the New Age. He said, "The technical achievements of science are obvious enough, its capacity to transform the life of scarcity into one of abundance, its invasion of many problems which have so far been the monopoly of philosophy in becoming more pronounced".[5]

Nehru popularised the scientific temper in the country and attacked superstitions and faith in astrology. He said, "It is the scientific approach, the adventures and yet critical temper of science, the search for truth and new knowledge, the refusal to accept any thing without testing and trial the capacity to change previous conclusions in the face of new evidence, the reliance on observed fact and not on pre-conceived theory, the hard discipline of the mind, all that is necessary; not merely for the application of science, but for life itself and the solution of its many problems".[6] From 1920 to 1964, there were very few important national and international issues on which he did not express himself. He spoke originally on mixed economy in India, the convergence of advanced capitalist and communist states, international action against discrimination based on racial distinction and the Asian-African resurgence and on the reconstruction of world peace.

Nehru gave a world perspective to India's struggle for independence and also he became the leading spokesman of the Congress party on world affairs. He was responsible for following up Gandhiji's South African movement for racial equality. He was also responsible for taking the Congress in a leftist direction and made strong socialist speeches which created a great impression, especially on the younger members of the Congress organisation. He was also responsible for bringing the People's Republic of China into the non-Communist world scenario first by giving recognition to the Chinese government and then by giving it prominence at the Afro-Asian Conference which met at Bandung in Indonesia. He was counted as a leader among the anti-fascist and anti-imperialist forces even when he was not a member of government. He gave the people the idea of planning the Indian economy by functioning as Chairman of the National Planning Committee appointed by the Congress when S.C. Bose was its President. He played a most important role in averting a Third World War by his policy of non-alignment and talking to both superpowers without at the same time aligning himself with either of them.[7]

Regarding Nehru's achievements, V.K.R.V. Rao said, "There is no doubt that Nehru's influence will extend far beyond his times and leave a lasting impact on our future generations. While not a professedly religious man like his master Gandhi, he was nevertheless essentially a Gandhian in his passion for peace, his belief in dialogue and persuasion, his absence of personal rancour or bitterness, his regard for human dignity, and his fundamental belief in the non-violent approach to all conflicts. At the same time, he was an embodiment of the modern spirit, with faith in reason and belief in science and the full confidence that the environment could be conquered and society reconstituted with the help of science and technology. This combination of the spiritual with the scientific, the old with the new, the inherited with the acquired, it is this unity in duality, of science and spirituality, that is likely to make the most lasting impact on the future generations of his fellow countrymen".

When Gandhi undertook a fast unto death for the untouchables, Nehru said, 'I felt annoyed with him for choosing a side issue for his final sacrifice. What would be the result of our freedom movement. . . . After so much sacrifice and brave endeavour, was our movement to tail off into something insignificant? I felt angry with him at his religious and sentimental approach to a political question and his frequent references to God in connection with it. He even seemed to suggest that God had indicated the very date of the fast. . . . So I thought and thought, while confusion reigned in my head, with anger and helplessness, and love for him who was cause of this upheaval. . . . And then a strange thing happened to me, I had quite an emotional crisis, and at the end of it I felt calmer, and the future seemed not so dark. Bapu had a curious knack of doing the right thing at the psychological moment, and it might be that his action would lead to great results, not only in the narrow field in which it was confined, but in the wider aspects of our national struggle". He was conscious of the influence that Gandhiji had on him, though he was not so happy with the changes that Gandhiji brought about in this thinking or action.

Nehru was not only a valiant fighter for the freedom of his country, a model of selfless devotion to a cause, and an indefatigable crusader for social justice but also a champion on the world stage of peaceful co-existence, of equality of nations, of dignity of the oppressed humanity, and of a world free of exploitation. He gave a new direction to the freedom struggle by integrating the Indian movement with the worldwide struggle against imperialism. In 1933, he said, "Whose freedom are we particularly striving for? There is the feudal India of the princes, the India of big zamindars, of small zamindars, of the professional classes, of the agriculturists, of the industrialists, of the bankers, of the lower middle class, of the workers. There are the interests of foreign capital and of those of home capital, of foreign services and of home services. . . . It is obvious that there are serious conflicts between the various interests in the country, and every law, every policy which is good for one interest may be harmful for another'. He did more than any leader for the struggle for independence to popularise socialist thinking and make it a part of the ethos of this struggle. His effort to draw up a plan for India's development in the midst of his heavy preoccupations, and in spite of enforced interruptions imposed by long periods of incarceration, even before the country had acquired the power to implement a plan so framed, was an instance of his devotion to and faith in the concept of planning.

Nehru is regarded as having shaped India's foreign policy after independence. He affirmed the dignity of all individuals, long denied to citizens of less favoured nations, irrespective of race and colour, and he worked for world peace. India may reverse the policies of Nehru and even discard the values that he taught and practised, but he will remain for generations to come, not only for India but for the whole world. He was prolific in his writings and he has given us more than a glimpse of his mind and his thought processes without a trace either of egoism or of self-pity. In his *Discovery of India*, he said, "We can make no complaint that life has traced us harshly for ours has been a willing choice, and perhaps life has not been so bad to us after all. For, only those can sense life who stand often on the verge of it, only those whose lives are not governed by the fear of death. In spite of all the mistakes we might have made, we have saved ourselves from triviality and an inner shame and cowardice".[8]

At the end of his love, Nehru gave all his life and strength to the liberation of mankind. In the *Discovery of India*, he said, "How amazing is the spirit of man! In spite of innumerable failings, man, throughout the ages, has sacrificed his life and all that he held dear for an ideal, for truth, for faith, for country and honour. That ideal may change but that capacity for self-sacrifice continues, and because of that, much may be forgiven to man, and it is impossible to lose hope for him. . . . Plaything of nature's mighty forces, less than the speak of dust in this vast universe, he has hurled defiance at the clemental powers, and with his mind, cradle of revolution, sought to master them. Whatever gods there be, there is something god-like in the man, as there is also something of the devil in him".[9] He was strongly attracted to the methods of science. He recognised that religion had supplied some deeply felt inner need of human nature, and that the vast majority of people all over the world could not do without some form of religious belief.

Nehru had little attraction for metaphysics. He said, "I have had a certain distaste for vague speculation. And yet I have sometimes found a certain intellectual fascination in trying to follow the rigid lines of metaphysical and philosophic thought of the ancients or the moderns. But I have never felt at ease there, and have escaped from their spell with a feeling of relief".[10] He had a remarkable receptivity to new thoughts and almost an obsessive aversion to dogmas.

Nehru was very characteristically an individual with a winning personality. He was a visionary with a practical side to his vision. The unifying spirit that governed his entire being and personality, his spirituality was the secret of Nehru's greatness. As a person, he stands out as an enlightened, brilliant, strong, and dynamic leader capable of rallying people to himself and to the cause. Lord Butler said, "He (Nehru) has all the makings of a dictator in him—vast popularity, a strong will, energy, pride ... and with all his love of the crowd, an intolerance of others, and a certain contempt for the weak and inefficient. His overwhelming desire to get things done, to sweep away what he dislikes and build anew, will hardly brook for long the slow processes of democracy".[11] The greatness of his soul made him extend his hand of friendship to all India's neighbours.

Gandhi recognised in Nehru a forceful spearhead of fervent nationalism and given the latter's acquaintance with the West and his knowledge of world affairs, cheerfully left to the young leader the enunciation and conduct of India's foreign policy. The upbringing of Nehru turned him into more of a Westerner than an Indian. He approached India almost as an alien critic, full of dislike for the present as well as for many relics of the past. He developed his rationalistic approach to the problems of life and his scientific attitude of mind. He dreamt of revolutionising the agricultural scene and, in the industrial area, of placing India in the forefront. In a spirit of Sarvodaya his compassion made him decide to give a preferential treatment to the scheduled castes and scheduled tribes. He sought to give religious minorities a feeling of security and a sense of belonging. He never understood the Gandhian concept of voluntary poverty in the interest of the development of the many. He had a romantic approach to life and development.

Nehru was a great believer in planned development. In this he drew his inspiration from Russia. Planning involves development of the various aspects of national life and economy such as improved agriculture, setting up new industries, extension of educational facilities, improvement of the machinery of administration fit to take up the responsibilities of development, evolution of a tax structure which will ensure social justice, land reforms, abolition of social inequalities and special measures for the uplift of women, backward castes and tribes and eradication of the colossal poverty concentrated in a large measure in the villages throughout the country. One of the major developments during his period was the development of scientific and technological institutions in India on a large scale. He was convinced that a technological revolution was necessary for the progress of the country, for greater production in agriculture and industry, for improving the health of the people both by preventive and curative methods for bettering communication and transport facilities and giving more employment for people. In the First Five-Year Plan, attention was given to the building up of a chain of national laboratories and other research institutions. In the Second Plan, research was made more broad-based and research facilities in universities and at other research centres were further extended. In the Third Plan the programme of scientific and technological research was further developed.[12]

One of the outstanding events during Nehru's period in Parliament was the foundation of India's foreign policy and the coming into existence of the non-aligned movement. To quote Nehru, "Having attained political freedom, we are earnestly desirous of removing the many ills that our country suffers from, of eliminating poverty and raising the standards of our people, and giving them full and equal opportunities of growth and advancement. I speak of India because it is my country. But many other countries in Asia tell the same story, for Asia today is resurgent and these countries, which long lay under foreign yoke have won back their independence and are fired by a new spirit to strive towards new ideals. To them, as to us independence is as vital as the breath they take to sustain life, and colonialism in any form, or anywhere is abhorrent. The vast strides that technology has made have brought a new age, of which the United States of America is the leader. Today, the whole world is our neighbour and the old divisions of continents and countries matter less and less. Peace and freedom have become indivisible. The preservation of peace forms the central aim of India's policy. It is in the pursuit of this policy that we have chosen the path of non-alignment in any military or like pact of alliance".

Again, on explaining the non-aligned movement, Nehru said, "Non-alignment does not mean passivity of mind or action, lack of faith or conviction. It does not mean submission to what we consider evil. It is a positive and dynamic approach to such problems that confront us. We believe that each country has not only the right to freedom, but also to decide its own policy and way of life. Only thus can true freedom flourish and a people grow according to their own genius. We believe, therefore, in non-aggression and non-interference by any country in the affairs of another, and the growth of tolerance between them and the capacity for peaceful coexistence. We think that, by the free exchange of ideas and trade and other contact between nations, each will learn from the other, and truth will prevail. We, therefore, endeavour to maintain friendly relations with all countries, even though we may disagree with them in their policies or structure of government. We think that, by this approach, we can serve not only our country, but also the larger causes of peace and good fellowship in the world".

With his faith in the assimilative capacity of India, Nehru visualised a secular India where all faiths and religions would be treated with equal respect. To him secularism was not a non-religious or irreligious secularism. It was, on the other hand, a secularism based on the flowering and flourishing of all religions in the country, on the concept of *Sarva Dharma Samabhaav*. This was a secularism suited to the psyche of the Indian people. It was a secularism acceptable to India where numerous religious movements had bloomed and which had an assimilative tradition of a thousand years. He claimed to be an agnostic and did not believe in religious ceremonies. He had great reverence and admiration for Buddha, Ramakrishna, and the Vedantic philosophy. He did scoff at religion. He said, "Probably it (religion) consists of the inner development of the individual, the evolution of his consciousness in a certain direction which is considered good. What that direction is will again be a matter for debate. But as far as I understand it, religion lays stress on this inner change and considers outward change as but the projection of this inner development. There can be no doubt that this development powerfully influences the outer environment".[13]

Nehru was responsible for making India a secular state. He tried to explain his idea of secularism in a circular to the Pradesh Congress Committee. On 5 August, 1954, he said, "Secularism meant freedom of religion and conscience, including freedom for those who have no religion. It means free play for all religions, subject only to their not interfering with each other'. Again he said, 'The word secular . . . conveys the idea of social and political equality. Thus a caste-ridden society is not properly secular. I have no desire to interfere with any person's belief, but when those beliefs became petrified in caste divisions, undoubtedly they affect the social structures of the state. They prevent us from realising the idea of equality which we claim to place before ourselves. They interfere in political matters, just as communalism interferes. We have opposed Communalism and continue to be stoutly opposed to it. Communalism means the dominance of one religious community. If that community is in a minority, this is opposed to all idea of democracy. But if that community is in a minority, dominance over others as a religious community would be wholly undemocratic'.

It is interesting to read Nehru's negative comments on religions and to see them balanced by positive insights that seem to reveal the man in a spiritual light. He said, "The spectacle of what is called religion or at any rate organised religion in India and elsewhere has filled me with horror. . . . Almost always it seems to stand for blind belief and reaction, dogma and bigotry, superstition and exploitation and the preservation of vested interests. And yet I knew well that there was something else in it (religion), something which supplied a deep inner craving of human beings and brought peace and comfort to innumerable tortured souls".[14] He bemoans the unduly other-worldly attitude of religion. He said, "The usual religious outlook does not concern itself with this world. . . . It is far removed from what I consider spirituality—the things of the spirit".[15] Again he said, "Religion probably consists of the inner development of the individual, the evolution of his consciousness. Religion lays stress on this inner change and considers outward changes as but the projection of this inner development". He saw the need for integration and said that obviously the outer environment also powerfully influences the inner development. He said, "A man who is the victim of economic circumstances and who is hedged and restricted by the struggle to live can very rarely achieve inner consciousness of any higher degree".[16]

Nehru was perhaps unconsciously enunciating a spirituality which must be practised in relation to the central concerns of society. A dynamic and action-oriented spirituality must become the true driving force of contemporary society. He nevertheless applied religion to life and practised the spirituality of purity of means, of non-violence, of positive mutual acceptance and respect for others and their opinions, a consistent consideration for others, even unselfish love, a great compassion for his suffering fellow Indians and fellow human beings, and an awesome sense of responsibility for improving the quality of life in society. To quote Homer A. Jack, "Spirituality is present in all people of goodwill; in theists as they imbue life with their experience of the divine presence and in atheists with their concern for the destiny of humanity. . . . Spirituality may be defined as the consciousness of responsibility rooted in one's experience of the divine".[17]

Nehru was a great democrat. His contribution in laying the firm foundation of Indian democracy and democratic institutions was a crucial one. In the formative years of our nationhood he towered over India like a colossus and yet he never brooked the thought of even anything remotely akin to dictatorship. A constitution which guarantees every citizen freedom; a Parliament which represents the voice of the people; a multi-party system which enriches democracy; an independent judiciary which affirms our faith in impartial dispensation of justice; a free press which chastises and rebukes the government—all these institutions owe a lot to the caring hand of Nehru and his vision of democratic India. He was a firm adherent of the democratic system. Intellectually also he was able to identify himself with the democratic way. As a believer in political dialogue, he concentrated on principles, ideas and programmes, and lifting debate well above personal differences. His attempt was always to convince, pursue, and cajole and not to impose upon, domineer or silence the opposition. He said that Parliamentary democracy demands many virtues. It demands, of course, ability. It demands a certain devotion to work. But it demands also a large measure of cooperations, of self-discipline, of restraint. His concern for the masses and the poor led him to socialism. He was of the opinion that socialism would not only help the poor to secure economic betterment but also to achieve a fuller and more satisfying life. He opined that socialism would help to wipe the tears from the eyes of the poorest of the poor and give to the poor security in the present and hope for the future.[18]

Nehru visualised and strove for a world free from strife, where the human being was free and could live with dignity. The message of peaceful co-existence was a voice of sanity in a world poised on the brink of self-destruction. The concept of non-alignment gave to international politics, a third force, which stood apart from the two power blocs and gradually gained in strength, fortified by the hopes and aspirations of millions of peace loving peoples all over the world. His firm belief in the dignity of the human being conditioned his perception of international affairs. Under the stewardship of Nehru, India was in the forefront of denouncing racialism and demanding stringent measures to isolate the racialist regime. He had visualised an India which would follow the path of democracy, socialism, secularism, and non-alignment.

Nehru's great contributions as a nation-builder and as a leader of international stature were born out of his intense patriotism, a pragmatic approach to India's national interest interpreted in an enlightened way, as he emphasised, an intuitively correct understanding of international situation, and his dynamics and a deep sense of humaneness, instead of ideological fanaticism. He became a man of the masses through his discipleship of Gandhiji. He was an institution builder—the democracy of India with all its imperfections is significantly his contribution, he was no great organiser. He had a vision of a world of multitude of decolonised nations and yet he displayed inadequate understanding of the role of power in that environment. He worked for international peace. He espoused centralised planning and passionately worked for accelerated development. His way of propagating his world-view was through his speeches in Parliament and other public forums. Though as a democrat he was tolerant of criticism, the sycophancy in the Indian political culture did not permit a debate on his world-view among his own partymen. His world-view was derived from the long Indian freedom struggle, from the Indian civilisational tradition, and from his interaction with the British society as it was in the process of democratisation. He was not a theoretician and had no doctrinaire pretensions.[19]

In 1949, Nehru said, "Independence consists fundamentally and basically of foreign relations. That is the test of independence. All else is local autonomy. Once foreign relations go out of your hands into the charge of somebody else to that extent and in that measure you are not independent".[20] Regarding India's role in world affairs, he said, "Forgetting present problems then for a while and looking ahead, India emerges as a strong united state, a federation of free units, intimately connected with her neighbours and playing an important part in world affairs. She is one of the very few countries which have the resources and capacity to stand on their own feet. Today probably the only such countries are the United States and the Soviet Union—China and India are potentially capable of joining that group. No other country, taken singly, apart from these four is actually or potentially in such a position. It is possible of course that larger federations or groups of nations may emerge in Europe or elsewhere and form huge multinational states. . . . Whatever happens, it will be well for the world if India can make her influence felt. For that influence will always be in favour of peace and cooperation and against aggression".[21]

Nehru was openly critical of the doctrine of balance of power as was expounded by the British historians. He also abhorred the doctrine of deterrence. Deterrence was abhorrent to him from both ethical and political points of view. His abhorrence of deterrence arose partly from Gandhiji's teaching that good ends could not be achieved except through good means and surely mass annihilation through nuclear weapons could not lead to any worthwhile end. He was a strong advocate of the 'One world' thesis and of international cooperation and being unaligned throwing India's weight behind world peace. His quest for international peace and cooperation and his constant rational pleas that a war among the major military blocs would put an end to human civilisation did not make him a pacifist. His democratic vision grew and blossomed in a congenial atmosphere provided by the long non-violent mass struggle for freedom under Gandhiji.

REFERENCES

1. Jawaharlal Nehru, *An Autobiography*, p. 591
2. *Ibid.*, p. 373.
3. Norman Dorothy, *Nehru: The First Fifty Years Presented in His Own Words*, p. 249.
4. Jawaharlal Nehru, *The Discovery of India*, pp. 16-17.
5. *Ibid.*
6. *Ibid.*, p. 525.
7. *Gandhi Marg*, 1989, pp. 564-565.
8. Jawaharlal Nehru, *The Discovery of India*, Last chapter.
9. *Ibid.*, p. 22.
10. *Ibid.*, p. 15.
11. Lord Butler, *First Nehru Memorial Lecture*, 1966.
12. *Gandhi Marg*, 1989, pp. 523-526.

13. Jawaharlal Nehru, *An Autobiography*, pp. 378-79.
14. *Ibid.*, p. 374.
15. *Ibid.*, p. 377.
16. *Ibid.*, p. 379.
17. Homer A. Jack, *Religion and the Struggle for World Community*, p. 124.
18. *Gandhi Marg*, 1989, pp. 557-558.
19. *Ibid.*, pp. 461-464.
20. *Jawaharlal Nehru's Speeches 1946-1949*, Vol. I, p. 242
21. Jawaharlal Nehru's *The Discovery of India*, p. 467

BIBLIOGRAPHY

Ahluwalia, R.K. and Shashi Ahluwalia, *Architects of Swaraj*, Intellectual Publishing House, Delhi, 1982.

Ahluwalia, B.K., *Facets of Nehru*, S.E.S. and Co., Delhi, 1967.

Alexander, G., *Jawaharlal Nehru*, Novosti Press Agency Publishing House, Moscow, 1989.

Bakshi, S.R., *Struggle for Independence, Jawaharlal Nehru*, Anmol Publications, Delhi, 1989.

Bali, D.R., *Modern Indian Thought*, Sterling Publishers Private Ltd., New Delhi, 1984.

Bharathi, K.S., *Gandhi and Nehru*, Indus Publishing Company, New Delhi, 1990.

Bhargava, G.S., *After Nehru: India's New Image*, Allied Publishers Pvt. Ltd., Bombay, 1966.

Bimal Prasad, *Gandhi, Nehru and J.P.*, Chanakya Publications, Delhi, 1985.

Brecher, M., *Nehru: A Political Biography*, Oxford University Press, London, 1959.

Bright, J.S., *Important Speeches of Jawaharlal Nehru*, Indian Printing Works, New Delhi, 1949.

Chaudhary, R., *Nehru in his own Works*, Navajeevan Publishing House, Ahmedabad, 1964.

Cousins, N., *Profiles of Nehru*, Indian Book Company, Delhi, 1966.

Das, M. N., *The Political Philosophy of Jawaharlal Nehru*, George Allen and Unwin Ltd., London, 1961.

Dutt, R.C., *Socialism of Jawaharlal Nehru*, Abhinav Publications, New Delhi, 1981.

Dutt, V., *Gandhi, Nehru and the Challenge*, Abhinav Publications, New Delhi, 1979.

Gajendragadkar, P.K., *Jawaharlal Nehru: A Glimpse of the Man and his Teachings*, Nagpur University, Nagpur, 1967.

Gopal, S., *Jawaharlal Nehru: A Biography*, Oxford University Press, Bombay, 1965.

Grover, V., *Political Thinkers of Modern India - Jawaharlal Nehru*, Deep and Deep Publications, New Delhi, 1990.

Gupta, S.K., *Gandhi-Jawaharlal Confluence*, Oriental Publishers, New Delhi, 1976.

Hutheesingh, K., *Nehru's Letters to His Sister*, Faber and Faber, London, 1963.

Jayaprakash Narayan, *Challenges After Nehru*, Sarvodaya Prachuralaya, Tanjore, 1964.

Karanjia, R.K., *The Mind of Mr. Nehru: An Interview*, George Allen and Unwin Ltd.; London, 1966.

Kripalani, K.R., *Gandhi Tagore and Nehru*, Hind Kitabs Ltd., Bombay, 1947.

Massey, I.P., *Nehruvian Constitutional Vision*, Deep and Deep Publications, New Delhi, 1991.

Mishra, D.P., *The Economic Philosophy of Pt. Jawaharlal Nehru*, Chugh Publications, 1978.

Moraes, F., *Jawaharlal Nehru: A Biography*, The Macmillan Co., New York, 1956.

Nanda, B.R., *Gokhale, Gandhi and the Nehrus*, St. Martin's Press, New York, 1973.

Nehru, J., *Glimpses of World History*, Kitabistan, Allahabad, 1935.

Nehru, J., *India and the World: Essays*, George Allen and Unwin Ltd., London, 1936.

Nehru, J., *The Discovery of India*, Asia Publishing House, Delhi, 1961.

Nehru, J., *An Autobiography*, The Bodley Head, London, 1953.

Nehru, J., *Before and After Independence*, The Indian Printing Works, New Delhi.

Nehru, J., *India: Today and Tomorrow*, Orient Longmans, 1960.

Rau, M.C., *Jawaharlal Nehru: Life and Work*, National Book Club, New Delhi, 1966.

Sarain, L.N., *Jawaharlal Nehru*, S. Chand and Co, Delhi, 1968

Saroj Prasad, *Nehru's Concept of Freedom*, Chugh Publications, Allahabad, 1989.

Sen, N.B., *Glorious Thoughts of Nehru*, New Book Society of India, New Delhi, 1968.

Singh, U., *Economic Thought of Indian Socialism*, Deep and Deep Publications, Delhi, 1985.

Singh, V.B., *Nehru on Socialism*, Publications Division, New Delhi, 1979.

Zakaria, R., *A Study of Nehru*, Hillary House Publications, Atlantic Highlands, 1960.

Journals

Gandhi Jyoti

Gandhi Marg

Harijan

Main Stream

INDEX